W9-AZM-251

CANDIDE

Voltaire

0052162

XXXX D

© 2002 by Spark Publishing

All rights reserved. No part of this publication may be reproduced, stored in a retrieval system, or transmitted, in any form or by any means, electronic, mechanical, photocopying, recording, or otherwise, without prior written permission from the publisher.

SPARKNOTES is a registered trademark of SparkNotes LLC.

Spark Publishing
A Division of Barnes & Noble
120 Fifth Avenue
New York, NY 10011
www.sparknotes.com

ISBN-13: 978-1-5866-3391-2
ISBN-10: 1-5866-3391-0

Please submit changes or report errors to www.sparknotes.com/errors.

Printed and bound in the United States

9   10   8

INTRODUCTION: STOPPING TO BUY SPARKNOTES ON A SNOWY EVENING

Whose words these are you *think* you know.
Your paper's due tomorrow, though;
We're glad to see you stopping here
To get some help before you go.

Lost your course? You'll find it here.
Face tests and essays without fear.
Between the words, good grades at stake:
Get great results throughout the year.

Once school bells caused your heart to quake
As teachers circled each mistake.
Use SparkNotes and no longer weep,
Ace every single test you take.

Yes, books are lovely, dark, and deep,
But only what you grasp you keep,
With hours to go before you sleep,
With hours to go before you sleep.

CONTENTS

NOTE: This SparkNote refers to the translation
by Robert M. Adams in the Norton Critical
Edition of *Candide* (New York: Norton, 1991).

CONTEXT

FRANÇOIS-MARIE AROUET, later known as Voltaire, was born in 1694 to a middle-class family in Paris. At that time, Louis XIV was king of France, and the vast majority of people in France lived in crushing poverty. When François-Marie came of age, the French aristocracy ruled with an iron fist. At the same time, however, the intellectual movement known as the Enlightenment was spreading ideas about the equality and basic rights of man and the importance of reason and scientific objectivity.

François-Marie received a Jesuit education at the college of Louis-le-Grand. Even as a child, his witty intelligence struck and sometimes outraged his teachers, setting the stage for his controversial writing career. François-Marie briefly worked as a secretary for the French Ambassador to Holland, but abandoned the position to devote himself to writing. As a writer, François-Marie soon became legendary throughout France for his sharp epigrams. His quick wit brought him fame, and with fame came a good deal of trouble. As a result of expressing his bitter, satirical wit at the expense of the French Regent, he was exiled from Paris to Sully, but through flattery he soon managed to have his exile rescinded. Shortly after returning to Paris, however, François was imprisoned in the Bastille for satirizing the government. While in prison, François assumed the pen name "Voltaire." Not long after his release in 1718, Voltaire's first play, *Oedipe*, was produced in Paris. At this point Voltaire was only twenty-four years old.

Voltaire moved in the circles of the rich and powerful. With his pen he alternately flattered and lambasted those around him, and this talent for biting satire earned him another stint in the Bastille in 1726. He was soon released on the condition that he move to England. Voltaire's exile in England was far from unpleasant, however, as a crowd of English literati received him with open arms. Within a matter of months, Voltaire became fluent in English, and English philosophy and society continued to fascinate him throughout his life. After three years he was allowed to return to France.

Voltaire's words attacked the church and the state with equal fervor, and earned him widespread repute. During his lifetime, trenchant writings attacking church or government were often attributed to him whether he had written them or not. A lifelong champion of the poor and downtrodden, he wrote against tyranny and religious persecution with unmatched audacity. Despite his relentless criticism of powerful individuals and institutions, Voltaire became good friends with King Frederick of Prussia. They often quarreled, as Voltaire inevitably quarreled with anyone in power, but the ties of their friendship were lasting.

In the 1750s, Voltaire grew increasingly appalled by the specters of injustice and inexplicable disaster that he saw around him. Many terrible events influenced his composition of *Candide*: a disastrous earthquake in Lisbon in 1755, about which he wrote a poem; the outbreak of the horrific Seven Years' War in the German states in 1756; and the unjust execution of the English Admiral John Byng in 1757, against which Voltaire spoke out. In 1759, Voltaire purchased Ferney, an estate near the border between France and Switzerland, so that he might easily flee across the border to escape French authorities. Ferney quickly became a retreat for important European intellectuals.

Published in 1759, *Candide* is considered Voltaire's signature work, and it is here that he levels his sharpest criticism against nobility, philosophy, the church, and cruelty. Though often considered a representative text of the Enlightenment, the novel actually savagely satires a number of Enlightenment philosophies and demonstrates that the Enlightenment was a far from monolithic movement.

In his later life Voltaire was involved in a wide variety of campaigns for social and political justice. When he returned to Paris at the age of eighty-three the populace hailed him with a hero's welcome. The strain of the trip was more than his failing health could support, however, and he died in May of 1778. Voltaire was buried in consecrated ground at Romilly-on-Seine, but in 1791 the National Assembly ordered his body entombed alongside René Descartes and other great French thinkers at the Panthéon in Paris. In 1814, religious fundamentalists stole the remains of Voltaire, as well as those of Jean-Jacques Rousseau, and dumped them in a pit full of quicklime, a "burial" reserved for individuals condemned and hated by the church. Voltaire would have appreciated the irony of this act, as he and Rousseau were bitter rivals during their lifetimes.

CANDIDE AND THE ENLIGHTENMENT

"The Enlightenment" is the name for a movement that encompasses a wide variety of ideas and advances in the fields of philosophy, science, and medicine that began in the seventeenth century and peaked in the eighteenth century. Many historians mark the French Revolution as the crowning event of the Enlightenment era. The primary feature of Enlightenment philosophy is a profound faith in the power of reason and rational thought to lead human beings to a better social structure. The political ideology of Enlightenment philosophers is characterized by a spirit of social reform. The champions of the Enlightenment called for rebellion against superstition, fear, and prejudice. They attacked the aristocracy and the church. *Candide* reflects Voltaire's lifelong aversion to Christian regimes of power and the arrogance of nobility, but it also criticizes certain aspects of the philosophical movement of the Enlightenment. It attacks the school of optimism that contends that rational thought can curtail the evils perpetrated by human beings.

Voltaire strongly opposed certain Enlightenment ideas about social class. Some Enlightenment thinkers promoted the idea of the enlightened monarch as an alternative to a radical reformation of society. Instead of denying the divine right of kings, the concept of the enlightened monarch relied on the idea that rulers could use their power to ensure the protection of their subjects' rights. The reach of the monarch's power could be extended so that he or she could ensure this protection. Thus, the name of the Enlightenment could be used to legitimize despotism. Moreover, witch-hunts and organized campaigns of religious persecution continued well into the eighteenth century, and Enlightenment philosophy's propagation of reason as a social antidote did not bring a halt to the ravages of superstition and fear. *Candide* illustrates this fact in the figure of the Grand Inquisitor who orders an auto-da-fé to ward off earthquakes, among many other examples. Voltaire's work may be difficult for the present-day student to understand because it alludes to some very specific concerns of his contemporaries. To better understand his wit as well as his relevant context, readers may benefit from consulting supplementary readings such as a history of the Enlightenment, a biography of Voltaire, or the writings of other Enlightenment thinkers like Rousseau and Leibniz.

CONTEXT

PLOT OVERVIEW

ANDIDE IS THE ILLEGITIMATE NEPHEW of a German baron. He grows up in the baron's castle under the tutelage of the scholar Pangloss, who teaches him that this world is "the best of all possible worlds." Candide falls in love with the baron's young daughter, Cunégonde. The baron catches the two kissing and expels Candide from his home. On his own for the first time, Candide is soon conscripted into the army of the Bulgars. He wanders away from camp for a brief walk, and is brutally flogged as a deserter. After witnessing a horrific battle, he manages to escape and travels to Holland.

In Holland, a kindly Anabaptist named Jacques takes Candide in. Candide runs into a deformed beggar and discovers that it is Pangloss. Pangloss explains that he has contracted syphilis and that Cunégonde and her family have all been brutally murdered by the Bulgar army. Nonetheless, he maintains his optimistic outlook. Jacques takes Pangloss in as well. The three travel to Lisbon together, but before they arrive their ship runs into a storm and Jacques is drowned. Candide and Pangloss arrive in Lisbon to find it destroyed by an earthquake and under the control of the Inquisition. Pangloss is soon hanged as a heretic, and Candide is flogged for listening with approval to Pangloss's philosophy. After his beating, an old woman dresses Candide's wounds and then, to his astonishment, takes him to Cunégonde. Cunégonde explains that though the Bulgars killed the rest of her family, she was merely raped and then captured by a captain, who sold her to a Jew named Don Isaachar. At present, she is a sex slave jointly owned by Don Isaachar and the Grand Inquisitor of Lisbon. Each of Cunégonde's two owners arrive in turn as she and Candide are talking, and Candide kills them both. Terrified, Candide, the old woman, and Cunégonde flee and board a ship bound for South America. During their journey, the old woman relates her own story. She was born the Pope's daughter but has suffered a litany of misfortunes that include rape, enslavement, and cannibalism.

Candide and Cunégonde plan to marry, but as soon as they arrive in Buenos Aires, the governor, Don Fernando, proposes to Cunégonde. Thinking of her own financial welfare, she accepts.

Authorities looking for the murderer of the Grand Inquisitor arrive from Portugal in pursuit of Candide. Along with a newly acquired valet named Cacambo, Candide flees to territory controlled by Jesuits who are revolting against the Spanish government. After demanding an audience with a Jesuit commander, Candide discovers that the commander is Cunégonde's brother, the baron, who also managed to escape from the Bulgars. Candide announces that he plans to marry Cunégonde, but the baron insists that his sister will never marry a commoner. Enraged, Candide runs the baron through with his sword. He and Cacambo escape into the wilderness, where they narrowly avoid being eaten by a native tribe called the Biglugs.

After traveling for days, Candide and Cacambo find themselves in the land of Eldorado, where gold and jewels litter the streets. This utopian country has advanced scientific knowledge, no religious conflict, no court system, and places no value on its plentiful gold and jewels. But Candide longs to return to Cunégonde, and after a month in Eldorado he and Cacambo depart with countless invaluable jewels loaded onto swift pack sheep. When they reach the territory of Surinam, Candide sends Cacambo to Buenos Aires with instructions to use part of the fortune to purchase Cunégonde from Don Fernando and then to meet him in Venice. An unscrupulous merchant named Vanderdendur steals much of Candide's fortune, dampening his optimism somewhat. Frustrated, Candide sails off to France with a specially chosen companion, an unrepentantly pessimistic scholar named Martin. On the way there, he recovers part of his fortune when a Spanish captain sinks Vanderdendur's ship. Candide takes this as proof that there is justice in the world, but Martin staunchly disagrees.

In Paris, Candide and Martin mingle with the social elite. Candide's fortune attracts a number of hangers-on, several of whom succeed in filching jewels from him. Candide and Martin proceed to Venice, where, to Candide's dismay, Cunégonde and Cacambo are nowhere to be found. However, they do encounter other colorful individuals there, including Paquette, the chambermaid-turned-prostitute who gave Pangloss syphilis, and Count Pococurante, a wealthy Venetian who is hopelessly bored with the cultural treasures that surround him. Eventually, Cacambo, now a slave of a deposed Turkish monarch, surfaces. He explains that Cunégonde is in Constantinople, having herself been enslaved along with the old woman. Martin, Cacambo, and Candide depart for Turkey, where Candide purchases Cacambo's freedom.

Candide discovers Pangloss and the baron in a Turkish chain gang. Both have actually survived their apparent deaths and, after suffering various misfortunes, arrived in Turkey. Despite everything, Pangloss remains an optimist. An overjoyed Candide purchases their freedom, and he and his growing retinue go on to find Cunégonde and the old woman. Cunégonde has grown ugly since Candide last saw her, but he purchases her freedom anyway. He also buys the old woman's freedom and purchases a farm outside of Constantinople. He keeps his longstanding promise to marry Cunégonde, but only after being forced to send the baron, who still cannot abide his sister marrying a commoner, back to the chain gang. Candide, Cunégonde, Cacambo, Pangloss, and the old woman settle into a comfortable life on the farm but soon find themselves growing bored and quarrelsome. Finally, Candide encounters a farmer who lives a simple life, works hard, and avoids vice and leisure. Inspired, Candide and his friends take to cultivating a garden in earnest. All their time and energy goes into the work, and none is left over for philosophical speculation. At last everyone is fulfilled and happy.

CHARACTER LIST

Candide The protagonist of the novel, Candide is a good-hearted but hopelessly naïve young man. His mentor, Pangloss, teaches him that their world is "the best of all possible worlds." After being banished from his adopted childhood home, Candide travels the world and meets with a wide variety of misfortunes, all the while pursuing security and following Cunégonde, the woman he loves. His faith in Pangloss's undiluted optimism is repeatedly tested. Candide is less a realistic character than a conduit for the attitudes and events that surround him. His opinions and actions are determined almost entirely by the influence of outside factors.

Pangloss Pangloss is a philosopher and Candide's tutor. His optimistic belief that this world is "the best of all possible worlds" is the primary target of the novel's satire. Pangloss's own experiences contradict this belief, but he remains faithful to it nonetheless. Like Candide, Pangloss is not a three-dimensional character. Instead, he is an exaggerated parody of overly optimistic Enlightenment philosophers.

Martin Martin is a cynical scholar whom Candide befriends as a travel companion. Martin has suffered a great deal in his life and preaches a philosophy of undiluted pessimism. More knowledgeable and intelligent than either Candide or Pangloss, Martin is nonetheless a flawed philosopher. Because he always expects nothing but the worst from the world, he often has trouble seeing the world as it really is.

Cunégonde Cunégonde is the daughter of a German baron who acts as Candide's benefactor until he discovers Candide's love for his daughter. Throughout much of the novel, Cunégonde is young and beautiful. After her father's castle is destroyed in war, a number of

CHARACTER LIST

exploitative men enslave her or use her as a mistress. Cunégonde returns Candide's love but is willing to betray him for the sake of her own interests. Like him, she is neither intelligent nor complex. Her very blandness casts a satiric light on Candide's mad romantic passion for her.

Cacambo Cacambo becomes Candide's valet when Candide travels in South America. A mixed-race native of the Americas, Cacambo is highly intelligent and morally honest. He is savvy and single-handedly rescues Candide from a number of scrapes. He is also directly responsible for Candide's reunion with Cunégonde. As a practical man of action, he stands in direct opposition to ineffectual philosophers such as Pangloss and Martin.

The old woman The old woman was born the daughter of a Pope. She has experienced the death of a fiancé, rape by pirates, slavery, and cannibalism in wartime. She becomes Cunégonde's servant. Her misfortunes have made her cynical about human nature, but she does not give in to self-pity. She is wise, practical, and loyal to her mistress. Though she has often been close to suicide, she always finds a reason to live.

The Commander or the baron The baron is Cunégonde's brother. After his family's castle is destroyed in wartime, he becomes a Jesuit priest. It is implied numerous times that he has homosexual tendencies. He is arrogant about his family's noble lineage and, though he is fond of the commoner Candide, he refuses to allow Candide to marry Cunégonde.

Jacques (the Anabaptist) Jacques is a humane Dutch Anabaptist. He cares for the itinerant Candide and Pangloss. Despite his kindness, Jacques is pessimistic about human nature. He drowns in the Bay of Lisbon while trying to save the life of an ungrateful sailor.

The farmer The farmer has a modest farm outside Constantinople. Candide and his friends are impressed with his lifestyle of hard work and simple pleasures, and adopt it for themselves.

Count Pococurante The count is a wealthy Venetian. He has a marvelous collection of art and literature, but he is bored with and critical of everything.

Paquette At the beginning of the novel, Paquette is the chambermaid of Cunégonde's mother. She has an affair with Pangloss and gives him syphilis. She eventually turns to prostitution to support herself. Brother Giroflée is one of her clients. In Venice, Candide is moved by Paquette's misery and gives her a large sum of money, which she quickly squanders.

Brother Giroflée Brother Giroflée is a dissatisfied monk. His parents forced him into a monastery to enlarge his brother's fortune. He pays for Paquette's services. Like her, he is miserable and does not get any happier after Candide gives him a large sum of money.

The Grand Inquisitor The Grand Inquisitor is an important figure in the Portuguese Catholic Church and represents the hypocrisy of religious leaders. He uses the threat of religious oppression to force the Jew Don Issachar to share Cunégonde with him. Meanwhile, he orders that suspected heretics be burned alive. Candide kills the Inquisitor when the Inquisitor discovers him with Cunégonde.

Don Issachar Don Issachar is a wealthy Jew. He purchases Cunégonde and makes her his mistress. The Grand Inquisitor forces him to share Cunégonde by threatening to burn him alive as a heretic. Candide kills Don Issachar when he interrupts Candide and Cunégonde.

Don Fernando d'Ibaraa y Figueora y Mascarenes y Lampourdos y Souza Don Fernando is the governor of Buenos Aires. He becomes infatuated with Cunégonde and makes her his mistress despite her engagement to Candide.

Vanderdendur Vanderdendur is a cruel slave owner and an unscrupulous merchant. After he steals one of Candide's jewel-laden sheep, his ship is sunk in a battle. Candide sees his death as a sign that retributive justice is at work in the world.

The Abbé of Perigord The abbé (abbot) is a Paris socialite who cheats Candide out of his money.

The Marquise of Parolignac The Marquise is a cunning, sexually licentious Paris socialite. She seduces Candide and steals some of his jeweled rings.

Analysis of Major Characters

Candide

Candide is the protagonist of the novel, but he is bland, naïve, and highly susceptible to the influence of stronger characters. Like the other characters, Candide is less a realistic individual than the embodiment of a particular idea or folly that Voltaire wishes to illustrate.

Candide's name is derived from the Latin word *candidus,* which means "white" and connotes fair-mindedness or a lack of corruption. As that name suggests, Candide begins the novel as a perfect innocent—wide-eyed in his worship of his tutor Pangloss's wrong-headed optimistic philosophy, and completely unfamiliar with the ways of the world. Over the course of the novel, Candide acquires wealth and even some knowledge about the world, and begins to question his faith in optimism. Yet that faith remains and is frequently reactivated by any event that pleases him, from the kindness of the stranger Jacques to the death of Vanderdendur, the merchant who cheats him. At the end of the novel, Candide rejects Pangloss's philosophizing in favor of the practical labor that is introduced to him by the old farmer. While this shift in philosophy appears on the surface to be real progress, Candide's personality remains essentially unchanged. He is still incapable of forming his own opinions, and has simply exchanged blind faith in Pangloss's opinions for blind faith in the opinions of the farmer. Despite his simplicity, Candide is an effective, sympathetic hero. He is fundamentally honest and good-hearted. He readily gives money to strangers like Brother Giroflée and the poorest deposed king, and he honors his commitment to marry Cunégonde even after his love for her has faded. His naïveté, though incredible, makes Candide sympathetic to readers; the world of the novel is exaggerated and fantastic, and we are likely to find the events described as unsettling and confusing as he does.

PANGLOSS

As Candide's mentor and a philosopher, Pangloss is responsible for the novel's most famous idea: that all is for the best in this "best of all possible worlds." This optimistic sentiment is the main target of Voltaire's satire. Pangloss's philosophy parodies the ideas of the Enlightenment thinker G. W. von Leibniz. Leibniz maintains that an all-good, all-powerful God had created the world and that, therefore, the world must be perfect. When human beings perceive something as wrong or evil, it is merely because they do not understand the ultimate good that the so-called evil is meant to serve. Like Candide, Pangloss is not a believable character; rather, he is a distorted, exaggerated representation of a certain kind of philosopher whose personality is inseparable from his philosophy.

Voltaire illustrates two major problems inherent in Pangloss's philosophy. First, his philosophy flies in the face of overwhelming evidence from the real world. Pangloss is ravaged by syphilis, nearly hanged, nearly dissected, and imprisoned, yet he continues to espouse optimism. He maintains his optimistic philosophy even at the end of the novel, when he himself admits that he has trouble believing in it. Voltaire advocates the induction of ideas from concrete evidence; Pangloss, in contrast, willfully ignores any evidence that contradicts his initial opinion. He also produces illogical arguments to support his preconceived notions, justifying the consumption of pork by saying that "since pigs were made to be eaten, we eat pork all year round."

Second, Pangloss's philosophy encourages a passive and complacent attitude toward all that is wrong in the world. If this world is the best one possible, than there is no reason to make any effort to change things perceived as evil or wrong. Therefore, when Pangloss's benefactor Jacques is drowning in the bay of Lisbon, Pangloss prevents Candide from trying to rescue him by "proving that the bay of Lisbon had been formed expressly for [Jacques] to drown in." The consequence of this mode of thinking is that, "while [Pangloss] was proving the point *a priori*, the vessel opened up and everyone perished."

MARTIN

Martin acts as both foil and counterpart to Pangloss. He is more believable than the other major characters in the novel, not because

CHARACTER ANALYSIS

he is more complex, but because he is more intelligent and more likely to draw conclusions with which we can identify. A scholar who has suffered personal and financial setbacks, Martin is as extreme a pessimist as Pangloss is an optimist. He even takes issue with Candide's statement that "there is some good" in the world. Direct experience plays a greater part in Martin's estimation of the world than it does in Pangloss's. As a result, he is able to provide insight into events far beyond Pangloss's ability to do so. Martin demonstrates such insight when he predicts that Giroflée and Paquette will not be happier for having money and when he analyzes the psychology of Count Pococurante.

Though Martin's philosophy is more effective and honest than Pangloss's, it also has some of the same flaws. While Martin is usually good at predicting how people will behave, he fails noticeably with Cacambo. Martin's absolute pessimism dictates that a valet trusted with millions in gold will certainly betray his master, yet Cacambo's honesty defies that pessimism. Voltaire prefers flexible philosophies based on real evidence to dogmatic assertions based on abstractions. Absolute optimism and absolute pessimism both fall into the latter category, because they will admit no exceptions. Like Pangloss, Martin abides by ideas that discourage any active efforts to change the world for the better. If, as Martin asserts, "man [is] bound to live either in convulsions of misery or in the lethargy of boredom," why should anyone try to rescue anyone else from "convulsions of misery"?

CACAMBO

Cacambo sheds a subtle and interesting light on the philosophical themes of the novel. Unlike any other character in the novel, he inspires perfect confidence, both in his intelligence and his moral uprightness. He knows both native American and European languages, and deals capably with both the Jesuits and the Biglugs. He suffers fewer gross misfortunes than any other character, less out of luck than because of his sharp wits, and he lives up to Candide's trust when Candide sends him to fetch Cunégonde. Any reader tempted to conclude that Voltaire has no faith in human nature must reconsider when faced with the example of Cacambo. Despite the optimism Cacambo inspires, however, he is no optimist himself. His wide experience of the world has led Cacambo to conclude that "the law of nature teaches us to kill our neighbor."

THEMES, MOTIFS & SYMBOLS

THEMES

Themes are the fundamental and often universal ideas explored in a literary work.

THE FOLLY OF OPTIMISM

Pangloss and his student Candide maintain that "everything is for the best in this best of all possible worlds." This idea is a reductively simplified version of the philosophies of a number of Enlightenment thinkers, most notably Gottfried Wilhelm von Leibniz. To these thinkers, the existence of any evil in the world would have to be a sign that God is either not entirely good or not all-powerful, and the idea of an imperfect God is nonsensical. These philosophers took for granted that God exists, and concluded that since God must be perfect, the world he created must be perfect also. According to these philosophers, people perceive imperfections in the world only because they do not understand God's grand plan. Because Voltaire does not accept that a perfect God (or any God) has to exist, he can afford to mock the idea that the world must be completely good, and he heaps merciless satire on this idea throughout the novel. The optimists, Pangloss and Candide, suffer and witness a wide variety of horrors—floggings, rapes, robberies, unjust executions, disease, an earthquake, betrayals, and crushing ennui. These horrors do not serve any apparent greater good, but point only to the cruelty and folly of humanity and the indifference of the natural world. Pangloss struggles to find justification for the terrible things in the world, but his arguments are simply absurd, as, for example, when he claims that syphilis needed to be transmitted from the Americas to Europe so that Europeans could enjoy New World delicacies such as chocolate. More intelligent and experienced characters, such as the old woman, Martin, and Cacambo, have all reached pessimistic conclusions about humanity and the world. By the novel's end, even Pangloss is forced to admit that he doesn't "believe a word of" his own previous optimistic conclusions.

THE USELESSNESS OF PHILOSOPHICAL SPECULATION

One of the most glaring flaws of Pangloss's optimism is that it is based on abstract philosophical argument rather than real-world evidence. In the chaotic world of the novel, philosophical speculation repeatedly proves to be useless and even destructive. Time and time again, it prevents characters from making realistic assessments of the world around them and from taking positive action to change adverse situations. Pangloss is the character most susceptible to this sort of folly. While Jacques drowns, Pangloss stops Candide from saving him "by proving that the bay of Lisbon had been formed expressly for this Anabaptist to drown in." While Candide lies under rubble after the Lisbon earthquake, Pangloss ignores his requests for oil and wine and instead struggles to prove the causes of the earthquake. At the novel's conclusion, Candide rejects Pangloss's philosophies for an ethic of hard, practical work. With no time or leisure for idle speculation, he and the other characters find the happiness that has so long eluded them. This judgment against philosophy that pervades *Candide* is all the more surprising and dramatic given Voltaire's status as a respected philosopher of the Enlightenment.

THE HYPOCRISY OF RELIGION

Voltaire satirizes organized religion by means of a series of corrupt, hypocritical religious leaders who appear throughout the novel. The reader encounters the daughter of a Pope, a man who as a Catholic priest should have been celibate; a hard-line Catholic Inquisitor who hypocritically keeps a mistress; and a Franciscan friar who operates as a jewel thief, despite the vow of poverty taken by members of the Franciscan order. Finally, Voltaire introduces a Jesuit colonel with marked homosexual tendencies. Religious leaders in the novel also carry out inhumane campaigns of religious oppression against those who disagree with them on even the smallest of theological matters. For example, the Inquisition persecutes Pangloss for expressing his ideas, and Candide for merely listening to them. Though Voltaire provides these numerous examples of hypocrisy and immorality in religious leaders, he does not condemn the everyday religious believer. For example, Jacques, a member of a radical Protestant sect called the Anabaptists, is arguably the most generous and humane character in the novel.

THE CORRUPTING POWER OF MONEY

When Candide acquires a fortune in Eldorado, it looks as if the worst of his problems might be over. Arrest and bodily injury are no longer threats, since he can bribe his way out of most situations. Yet, if anything, Candide is *more* unhappy as a wealthy man. The experience of watching his money trickle away into the hands of unscrupulous merchants and officials tests his optimism in a way that no amount of flogging could. In fact, Candide's optimism seems to hit an all-time low after Vanderdendur cheats him; it is at this point that he chooses to make the pessimist Martin his traveling companion. Candide's money constantly attracts false friends. Count Pococurante's money drives him to such world-weary boredom that he cannot appreciate great art. The cash gift that Candide gives Brother Giroflée and Paquette drives them quickly to "the last stages of misery." As terrible as the oppression and poverty that plague the poor and powerless may be, it is clear that money—and the power that goes with it—creates at least as many problems as it solves.

MOTIFS

Motifs are recurring structures, contrasts, or literary devices that can help to develop and inform the text's major themes.

RESURRECTION

At various points, Candide believes that Cunégonde, Pangloss, and the baron are dead, only to discover later that they have actually survived the traumas that should have killed them. The function of these "resurrections" in the novel is complicated. On the one hand, they seem to suggest a strange, fantastic optimism that is out of step with the general tone of the novel. Death, the only misfortune from which one would never expect a character to recover, actually proves to be "reversible." On the other hand, the characters who get "resurrected" are generally those whose existence does more harm than good. Each "resurrected" figure embodies a harmful aspect of human nature: Cunégonde reveals the shallowness of beauty and fickleness of love, Pangloss's optimism represents folly, and the baron's snobbery represents arrogance and narrow-minded social oppression. Through these characters' miraculous resurrections, Voltaire may be trying to tell his readers that these traits never die.

RAPE AND SEXUAL EXPLOITATION

Candide is full of uncommonly graphic accounts of the sexual exploitation of women. The three main female characters—Cunégonde, the old woman, and Paquette—are all raped, forced into sexual slavery, or both. Both the narrator's and the characters' attitudes toward these events are strikingly nonchalant and matter-of-fact. Voltaire uses these women's stories to demonstrate the special dangers to which only women are vulnerable. Candide's chivalric devotion to Cunégonde, whom he wrongly perceives as a paragon of female virtue, is based on willful blindness to the real situation of women. The male characters in the novel value sexual chastity in women but make it impossible for women to maintain such chastity, exposing another hypocritical aspect of Voltaire's Europe.

POLITICAL AND RELIGIOUS OPPRESSION

Candide witnesses the horrors of oppression by the authorities of numerous states and churches. Catholic authorities burn heretics alive, priests and governors extort sexual favors from their female subjects, businessmen mistreat slaves, and Candide himself is drafted into and abused in the army of the Bulgar king. Even the English government, which Voltaire admired, executes an admiral for the "crime" of fighting with insufficient audacity against the French. Powerful institutions seem to do no good—and instead, much harm—to their defenseless subjects. Voltaire himself protested loudly against political injustice throughout his life. The characters in *Candide,* however, choose a different route. Shortly after hearing about the politically motivated killings of several Turkish officials, they take the old farmer's advice and decide to ignore the injustices that surround them, channeling their wealth and energy instead into the simple labors that bring them happiness.

SYMBOLS

Symbols are objects, characters, figures, or colors used to represent abstract ideas or concepts.

PANGLOSS

Pangloss is less a well-rounded, realistic character than a symbol of a certain kind of philosopher. His optimism and logical fallacies are meant to represent the thought of G.W. von Leibniz and other Enlightenment thinkers. He is an open symbol of the folly both of blind optimism and of excessive abstract speculation.

THE GARDEN

At the end of the novel, Candide and his companions find happiness in raising vegetables in their garden. The symbolic resonance of the garden is rich and multifaceted. As Pangloss points out, it is reminiscent of the Garden of Eden, in which Adam and Eve enjoyed perfect bliss before their fall from God's grace. However, in *Candide* the garden marks the end of the characters' trials, while for Adam and Eve it is the place where their troubles begin. Moreover, in the Garden of Eden Adam and Eve enjoyed the fruits of nature without having to work, whereas the main virtue of Candide's garden is that it forces the characters to do hard, simple labor. In the world outside the garden, people suffer and are rewarded for no discernible cause. In the garden, however, cause and effect are easy to determine—careful planting and cultivation yield good produce. Finally, the garden represents the cultivation and propagation of life, which, despite all their misery, the characters choose to embrace.

THE LISBON EARTHQUAKE

The earthquake in *Candide* is based on a real earthquake that leveled the city of Lisbon in 1755. Before writing *Candide,* Voltaire wrote a long poem about that event, which he interpreted as a sign of God's indifference or even cruelty toward humanity. The earthquake represents all devastating natural events for which no reasonable justification can be found, though thinkers like Pangloss might do their best to fabricate flimsy justifications in order to maintain a philosophical approach to life.

Summary & Analysis

Chapters 1–4

Summary: Chapter 1

> ... *those who say everything is well are uttering mere*
> *stupidities; they should say everything is for the best.*
> (See QUOTATIONS, p. 51)

Candide lives in the castle of the baron of Thunder-ten-tronckh in Westphalia. Candide is the illegitimate son of the baron's sister. His mother refused to marry his father because his father's family tree could only be traced through "seventy-one quarterings." The castle's tutor, Pangloss, teaches "metaphysico-theologo-cosmolonigology" and believes that this world is the "best of all possible worlds." Candide listens to Pangloss with great attention and faith. Miss Cunégonde, the baron's daughter, spies Pangloss and a maid, Paquette, engaged in a lesson in "experimental physics." Seized with the desire for knowledge, she hurries to find Candide. They flirt and steal a kiss behind a screen. The baron catches them and banishes Candide.

Summary: Chapter 2

Candide wanders to the next town, where two men find him half-dead with hunger and fatigue. They give him money, feed him, and ask him to drink to the health of the king of the Bulgars. They then conscript him to serve in the Bulgar army, where Candide suffers abuse and hardship as he is indoctrinated into military life. When he decides to go for a walk one morning, four soldiers capture him and he is court-martialed as a deserter. He is given a choice between execution and running the gauntlet (being made to run between two lines of men who will strike him with weapons) thirty-six times. Candide tries to choose neither option by arguing that "the human will is free," but his argument is unsuccessful. He finally chooses to run the gauntlet.

After running the gauntlet twice, Candide's skin is nearly flayed from his body. The king of the Bulgars happens to pass by. Discovering that Candide is a metaphysician and "ignorant of the world," the king pardons him. Candide's wounds heal in time for him to serve in a war between the Bulgars and the Abares.

SUMMARY: CHAPTER 3

The war results in unbelievable carnage, and Candide deserts at the first opportunity. In both kingdoms he sees burning villages full of butchered and dying civilians.

Candide escapes to Holland, where he comes upon a Protestant orator explaining the value of charity to a crowd of listeners. The orator asks Candide whether he supports "the good cause." Remembering Pangloss's teachings, Candide replies that "[t]here is no effect without a cause." The orator asks if Candide believes that the Pope is the Antichrist. Candide explains that he does not know, but that in any case he is hungry and must eat. The orator curses Candide and the orator's wife dumps human waste over Candide's head. A kind Anabaptist, Jacques, takes Candide into his home and employs Candide in his rug factory. Jacques's kindness revives Candide's faith in Pangloss's theory that everything is for the best in this world.

SUMMARY: CHAPTER 4

Candide finds a deformed beggar in the street. The beggar is Pangloss. Pangloss tells Candide that the Bulgars attacked the baron's castle and killed the baron, his wife, and his son, and raped and murdered Cunégonde. Pangloss explains that syphilis, which he contracted from Paquette, has ravaged his body. Still, he believes that syphilis is necessary in the best of worlds because the line of infection leads back to a man who traveled to the New World with Columbus. If Columbus had not traveled to the New World and brought syphilis back to Europe, then Europeans would also not have enjoyed New World wonders such as chocolate.

Jacques finds a doctor to cure Pangloss, who loses an eye and an ear to the syphilis. Jacques hires Pangloss as his bookkeeper and then takes Candide and Pangloss on a business trip to Lisbon. Jacques disagrees with Pangloss's assertion that this is the best of worlds and claims that "men have somehow corrupted Nature." God never gave men weapons, he claims, but men created them "in order to destroy themselves."

ANALYSIS: CHAPTERS 1–4

Voltaire satirizes virtually every character and attitude he portrays. The name of the barony—Thunder-ten-tronckh, a guttural, primitive-sounding set of words—undercuts the family's pride in their noble heritage. Throughout *Candide* Voltaire mocks the aristocracy's belief in "natural" superiority by birth. The baron's sister, for instance, has refused to marry Candide's father because he only had seventy-one quarterings (noble lineages) in his coat of arms, while her own coat of arms had seventy-two. This exaggeration, a classic tool of satire, makes the nobility's concern over the subtleties of birth look absurd. Voltaire uses exaggeration of this sort throughout the novel to expose the irrationality of various beliefs—and, more importantly, the irrationality of pursuing any belief to an extreme degree.

Pangloss is a parody of all idle philosophers who debate subjects that have no real effect on the world. The name of his school of thought, metaphysico-theologo-cosmolo-nigology, pokes fun at Pangloss's verbal acrobatics and suggests how ridiculous Voltaire believes such idle thinkers to be. More specifically, critics agree that Pangloss's optimistic philosophy parodies the ideas of G.W. von Leibniz, a seventeenth-century mathematician and philosopher who claimed that a pre-determined harmony pervaded the world. Both Pangloss and Leibniz claim that this world must be the best possible one, since God, who is perfect, created it. Human beings perceive evil in the world only because they do not understand the greater purpose that these so-called evil phenomena serve. Leibniz's concept of the world is part of a larger intellectual trend called theodicy, which attempts to explain the existence of evil in a world created by an all-powerful, perfectly good God. Voltaire criticizes this school of philosophical thought for its blind optimism, an optimism that appears absurd in the face of the tragedies the characters in *Candide* endure.

At the beginning of the novel, Candide's education consists only of what Pangloss has taught him. His expulsion from the castle marks Candide's first direct experience with the outside world, and thus the beginning of his re-education. Candide's experiences in the army and the war directly contradict Pangloss's teaching that this world is the best of all possible worlds. The world of the army is full of evil, cruelty, and suffering. Powerful members of the nobility start wars, but common soldiers and subjects suffer the consequences. Neither side of the conflict is better than the other, and both engage in rape, murder, and destruction.

In his attacks on religious hypocrisy, Voltaire spares neither Protestants nor Catholics. The Dutch orator embodies the pettiness of clergy members who squabble over theological doctrine while people around them suffer the ravages of war, famine, and poverty. The orator cares more about converting his fellow men to his religious views than about saving them from real social evils.

The Anabaptist Jacques is a notable exception. The Anabaptists are a Protestant sect that rejects infant baptism, public office, and worldly amusements. The Amish and the Mennonites, for example, follow Anabaptist doctrine. Voltaire, generally skeptical of religion, was unusually sympathetic to Anabaptist beliefs. Jacques is one of the most generous and human characters in the novel, but he is also realistic about human faults. He acknowledges the greed, violence, and cruelty of mankind, yet still offers kind and meaningful charity to those in need. Unlike Pangloss, a philosopher who hesitates when the world requires him to take action, Jacques both studies human nature and acts to influence it—a combination that Voltaire apparently sees as ideal but extremely rare.

CHAPTERS 5–10

SUMMARY: CHAPTER 5

A furious storm overtakes Candide's ship on its way to Lisbon. Jacques tries to save a sailor who has almost fallen overboard. He saves the sailor but falls overboard himself, and the sailor does nothing to help him. The ship sinks, and Pangloss, Candide, and the sailor are the only survivors. They reach shore and walk toward Lisbon.

Lisbon has just experienced a terrible earthquake and is in ruins. The sailor finds some money in the ruins and promptly gets drunk and pays a woman for sex. Meanwhile the groans of dying and buried victims rise from the ruins. Pangloss and Candide help the wounded, and Pangloss comforts the victims by telling them the earthquake is for the best. One of the officers of the Inquisition accuses Pangloss of heresy because an optimist cannot possibly believe in original sin. The fall and punishment of man, the Catholic Inquisitor claims, prove that everything is not for the best. Through some rather twisted logic, Pangloss attempts to defend his theory.

SUMMARY: CHAPTER 6

The Portuguese authorities decide to burn a few people alive to prevent future earthquakes. They choose one man because he has married his godmother, and two others because they have refused to eat bacon (thus presumably revealing themselves to be Jewish). The authorities hang Pangloss for his opinions and publicly flog Candide for "listening with an air of approval." When another earthquake occurs later the same day, Candide finds himself doubting that this is the best of all possible worlds.

SUMMARY: CHAPTER 7

Just then an old woman approaches Candide, treats his wounds, gives him new clothes, and feeds him. After two days, she leads him to a house in the country to meet his real benefactor, Cunégonde.

SUMMARY: CHAPTER 8

Cunégonde explains to Candide that the Bulgars have killed her family. After executing a soldier whom he found raping Cunégonde, a Bulgar captain took Cunégonde as his mistress and later sold her to a Jew, Don Issachar. After seeing her at Mass, the Grand Inquisitor wanted to buy her from Don Issachar; when Don Issachar refused, the Grand Inquisitor threatened him with auto-da-fé (burning alive). The two agreed to share Cunégonde; the Grand Inquisitor would have her four days a week, Don Issachar the other three. Cunégonde was present to see Pangloss hanged and Candide whipped, the horror of which made her doubt Pangloss's teachings. Cunégonde told the old woman, her servant, to care for Candide and bring him to her.

SUMMARY: CHAPTER 9

Don Issachar arrives to find Cunégonde and Candide alone together, and attacks Candide in a jealous rage. Candide kills Don Issachar with a sword given to him by the old woman. The Grand Inquisitor arrives to enjoy his allotted time with Cunégonde and is surprised to find Candide. Candide kills him. Cunégonde gathers her jewels and three horses from the stable and flees with Candide and the old woman. The Holy Brotherhood gives the Grand Inquisitor a grand burial, but throws Don Issachar's body on a dunghill.

SUMMARY: CHAPTER 10

A Franciscan friar steals Cunégonde's jewels. Despite his agreement with Pangloss's philosophy that "the fruits of the earth are a common heritage of all," Candide nonetheless laments the loss. Candide and Cunégonde sell one horse and travel to Cadiz, where they find troops preparing to sail to the New World. Paraguayan Jesuit priests have incited an Indian tribe to rebel against the kings of Spain and Portugal. Candide demonstrates his military experience to the general, who promptly makes him a captain. Candide takes Cunégonde, the old woman, and the horses with him, and predicts that it is the New World that will prove to be the best of all possible worlds. But Cunégonde claims to have suffered so much that she has almost lost all hope. The old woman admonishes Cunégonde for complaining because Cunégonde has not suffered as much as she has.

ANALYSIS: CHAPTERS 5–10

Readers have proposed various interpretations of Jacques's death. His death could represent Voltaire's criticism of the optimistic belief that evil is always balanced by good. Jacques, who is good, perishes while saving the sailor, who is selfish and evil; the result is not a balance but a case of evil surviving good. Jacques's death could also represent the uselessness of Christian values. Continually referred to as "the Anabaptist," Jacques is an altruist who does not change society for the better; he ends up a victim of his own altruism.

Pangloss responds to Jacques's death by asserting that the bay outside Lisbon had been formed "expressly for this Anabaptist to drown in." This argument is a parody of the complacent reasoning of optimistic philosophers. Convinced that the world God created must necessarily be perfectly planned and executed, optimists end up drawing far-fetched and unlikely connections between apparently unrelated events, such as the formation of a bay and the drowning of Jacques.

Voltaire bases the earthquake in *Candide* on an actual historical event that affected him deeply. A devastating earthquake on November 1, 1755—All Saints' Day—leveled Lisbon and killed over 30,000 people, many of whom died while praying in church. The earthquake challenged a number of Enlightenment thinkers' optimistic views of the world.

The sailor's debauchery amid the groans of the wounded represents indifference in the face of evil. Voltaire strongly condemned indifference, and his belief that human inaction allows suffering to continue is evident in his depictions of the sailor and Pangloss. At one point, when Candide is knocked down by rubble and begs Pangloss to bring him wine and oil, Pangloss ignores Candide's request and rambles on about the causes and ultimate purpose of the earthquake. Voltaire proposes a fundamental similarity between Pangloss's behavior and the sailor's actions. The sailor's sensual indulgence in the face of death is grotesque and inhumane. While less grotesque, Pangloss's philosophizing is no better, because it too gets in the way of any meaningful, useful response to the disaster.

The auto-da-fé, or act of faith, was the Inquisition's practice of burning heretics alive. Beginning in the Middle Ages, the officials of the Inquisition systematically tortured and murdered tens of thousands of people on the slightest suspicion of heresy against orthodox Christian doctrine. Jews, Protestants, Muslims, and accused witches were victims of this organized campaign of violence. Like many Enlightenment intellectuals, Voltaire was appalled by the barbarism and superstition of the Inquisition, and by the religious fervor that inspired it.

Voltaire makes his ideological priorities clear in *Candide*. Pangloss's philosophy lacks use and purpose, and often leads to misguided suffering, but the Inquisition's determination to suppress dissenting opinion at any cost represents tyranny and unjust persecution. The Inquisition authorities twist Pangloss's words to make them appear to be a direct attack on Christian orthodoxy, and flog Candide for merely *seeming* to approve of what Pangloss says. This flogging of Candide represents exaggeration on Voltaire's part, an amplification of the Inquisition's repressive tactics that serves a satirical purpose. Along with outrage at the cruelty of the Inquisition, we are encouraged to laugh at its irrationality, as well as at the exaggerated nature of Candide's experience.

Cunégonde's situation inspires a similarly subversive combination of horror and absurdity. Her story demonstrates the vulnerability of women to male exploitation and their status as objects of possession and barter. Cunégonde is bought and sold like a painting or piece of livestock, yet the deadpan calm with which she relates her experiences to Candide creates an element of the absurd. Candide takes this absurdity further; as Cunégonde describes how her Bulgar rapist left a wound on her thigh, Candide interrupts to say, "What a pity! I should very much like to see it." In the middle of this litany of dreadful events, Candide's suggestive comments seem ridiculous, but the absurdity provides comic relief from the despicably violent crimes that Cunégonde describes.

The stereotyped representation of the Jew Don Issachar may offend the contemporary reader, but it demonstrates the hypocrisy that afflicted even such a progressive thinker as Voltaire. Voltaire attacked religious persecution throughout his life, but he suffered from his own collection of prejudices. In theory, he opposed the persecution of Jews, but in practice, he expressed anti-Semitic views of his own. In his *Dictionary of Philosophy,* Voltaire describes the Jews as "the most abominable people in the world." Don Issachar's character is a narrow, mean-spirited stereotype—a rich, conniving merchant who deals in the market of human flesh.

Voltaire makes another attack on religious hypocrisy through the character of the Franciscan who steals Cunégonde's jewels. The Franciscan order required a vow of poverty from its members, making Voltaire's choice of that order for his thief especially ironic.

CHAPTERS 11–13

SUMMARY: CHAPTER 11

The old woman tells her story. It turns out that she is the daughter of Pope Urban X and the princess of Palestrina. She was raised in the midst of incredible wealth. At fourteen, already a stunning beauty, she was engaged to the prince of Massa Carrara. The two of them loved another passionately. However, during the lavish wedding celebration, the prince's mistress killed the prince with a poisoned drink, and the old woman and her mother set sail to mourn at their estate in Gaeta. On the way, pirates boarded the ship and the pope's soldiers surrendered without a fight. The pirates examined every bodily orifice of their prisoners, searching for hidden jewels. They raped the women and sailed to Morocco to sell them as slaves.

A civil war was underway in Morocco, and the pirates were attacked. The old woman saw her mother and their maids of honor ripped apart by the men fighting over them. After the fray ended, the old woman climbed out from under a heap of dead bodies and crawled to rest under a tree. She awoke to find an Italian eunuch vainly attempting to rape her.

SUMMARY: CHAPTER 12

> *A hundred times I wanted to kill myself, but always I*
> *loved life more.*   (See QUOTATIONS, p. 53)

The old woman continues her story. Despite the eunuch's attempt to rape her, she was delighted to encounter a countryman, and the eunuch carried her to a nearby cottage to care for her. They discovered that he had once served in her mother's palace. The eunuch promised to take the old woman back to Italy, but then took her to Algiers and sold her to the prince as a concubine.

The plague swept through Algiers, killing the prince and the eunuch. The old woman was subsequently sold several times and ended up in the hands of a Muslim military commander. He took his seraglio with him when ordered to defend the city of Azov against the Russians. The Russians leveled the city, and only the commander's fort was left standing. Desperate for food, the officers killed and ate two eunuchs. They planned to do the same with the women, but a "pious and sympathetic" religious leader persuaded them to merely cut one buttock from each woman for food. Eventually, the Russians killed all the officers.

The women were taken to Moscow. A nobleman took the old woman as his slave and beat her daily for two years. He was executed for "court intrigue," and the old woman escaped. She worked as a servant in inns across Russia. She came close to suicide many times in her life, but never carried it out because she "loved life" too much. The old woman wonders why human nature makes people want to live even though life itself is so often a curse. She tells Candide and Cunégonde to ask each passenger on the ship to tell his story. She wagers that every single one has been upset to be alive.

SUMMARY: CHAPTER 13

At the old woman's urging, Candide and Cunégonde ask their fellow passengers about their experiences. They find that the old woman's prediction is correct. When the ship docks at Buenos Aires, they visit the haughty, self-important governor, Don Fernando d'Ibaraa y Figueora y Mascarenes y Lampourdos y Souza, who orders Candide to review his company. When Candide leaves, Don Fernando begs Cunégonde to marry him. The shrewd old woman advises Cunégonde to marry the governor, as marrying him could make both her and Candide's fortune.

Meanwhile, a Portuguese official and police arrive in the city. It turns out that when the Franciscan who stole Cunégonde's jewels tried to sell them, the jeweler recognized them as belonging to the Grand Inquisitor. Before he was hanged, the Franciscan described the three people from whom he stole the jewels—ostensibly the Grand Inquisitor's murderers. The authorities sent the Portuguese official to capture these three. The old woman advises Cunégonde to remain in Buenos Aires, since Candide was responsible for the murder and the governor will not allow the authorities to do Cunégonde any harm. The old woman advises Candide to flee immediately.

ANALYSIS: CHAPTERS 11–13

The old woman's story serves a dual purpose. The catalogue of her sufferings illustrates a vast array of human evils that contradict Pangloss's optimistic view of the world. She has lived through violence, rape, slavery, and betrayal and seen the ravages of war and greed.

The old woman's story also functions as a criticism of religious hypocrisy. She is the daughter of the Pope, the most prominent member of the Catholic Church. The Pope has not only violated his vow of celibacy, but has also proven unable and unwilling to protect his daughter from the misfortunes that befell her.

The officers who eat the old woman's buttock value the integrity of their military oath more highly than the lives of the eunuchs and women inside their fort. Their behavior demonstrates the folly of absurd adherence to an outmoded system of belief. Even after it is clear that their side has no hope of winning the war, the officers choose to practice cannibalism rather than betray their oath. This choice undermines their lofty concepts of honor and duty, and makes even the cleric, who advocates mutilation rather than execution, appear humane.

Figures such as the cleric, who perform "good" deeds that are somehow compromised, limited, or otherwise ineffective, turn up throughout the novel and are often presented comically or ironically. Another example is the kindly French surgeon who treats the women's wounds but does nothing to prevent them from being sold to new slave owners. The surgeon's "enlightened" practice of medicine does nothing to alleviate the women's real suffering. He merely helps the women survive to encounter more misery and injustice.

The old woman is pessimistic but acutely aware of the world she lives in. Direct experience dictates her worldview, and her pragmatism lends her more wisdom and credibility than any of her travel companions. The old woman chides Cunégonde for making judgments about the world based on her limited experience, and urges Candide and Cunégonde to gather knowledge through investigation before making judgments. Through her character, Voltaire reiterates the importance of actual, verifiable evidence and the limited value of judgments based on empty philosophical rhetoric. *speaking + writing effectively*

The old woman defines life as misery, but unlike her younger companions she is not prone to self-pity. She tells Cunégonde, "I would not even have mentioned my own misfortunes, if you had not irked me a bit, and if it weren't the custom, on shipboard, to pass the time with stories." For her, tales of woe are neither edifying nor moving. They are simply a way of making a point and staving off boredom. Though her suffering does not move her to self-pity, it does shape the pragmatism and frankness that define her character.

The old woman's meditations on suicide speak to one of the *not essential* novel's most pressing underlying concerns. If life is so full of unmitigated suffering, the prospect of taking one's own life seems a reasonable option. The old woman, a Pope's daughter, does not even consider the standard Christian mandate that suicide is a sin and that those who commit it are destined to burn in hell. Despite her pessimism, the old woman's speech on this subject has a strange ✓ hopefulness to it. She asserts that people cling to life because they *→ declare* love it, not because they fear eternal punishment. Human beings *doctorine that evil overbalances happiness in life.* naturally embrace life—a stupid move, perhaps, but one that demonstrates passion, strong will, and an almost heroic endurance. *withstand hardship*

Don Fernando represents a satire on the arrogance of the nobility. His long list of names mocks the importance that the nobility *attitude of superiority* attaches to titles. Here, Voltaire once again attacks the nobility's belief that it is naturally endowed with superior virtues that entitle it *morally excellent* to wealth and power. Rather than being a wise or just governor, Don Fernando is a predator, a liar, a cheat, and a joke.

Cunégonde's decision to accept Don Fernando's proposal adds greater complexity to her character. She is the object of Candide's lust and idealistic devotion, and Voltaire repeatedly refers to her as "the lovely Cunégonde." But she is far from the semi-divine romantic heroine Candide believes her to be, and her calculating, self-serving decision to marry the Don is proof of this. Voltaire undercuts Candide's romantic ideals by having him continue to worship Cunégonde even after she faithlessly marries the Don. It is possible that Voltaire also uses these ideals to emphasize Cunégonde's lack of chastity, although it is unlikely that Voltaire means to condemn her for this. Cunégonde uses her beauty and sexuality to manipulate men, which seems a highly reasonable way of behaving in a world in which sexuality is the only asset women possess.

CHAPTERS 14–16

SUMMARY: CHAPTER 14

Candide's new valet Cacambo is fond of his master and urges Candide to follow the old woman's advice. Cacambo tells Candide not to worry about Cunégonde because God always takes care of women. Cacambo suggests that they fight on the side of the rebellious Paraguayan Jesuits. The two reach the rebel guard and ask to speak to the colonel, but the colonel orders their weapons and their horses seized. A sergeant tells Candide and Cacambo that the colonel does not have time to see them and that the Father Provincial hates Spaniards. He gives them three hours to get out of the province. Cacambo informs the sergeant that Candide is German. The colonel agrees to see him.

Candide and Cacambo are led to the colonel's lavish pavilion. Their weapons and horses are returned. It turns out that the colonel is Cunégonde's brother, now the baron of Thunder-ten-tronckh. Candide and the baron embrace one another in tearful joy. Candide reports that Cunégonde also survived the attack and that she is with the governor. While they wait for the Father Provincial, the colonel tells his story.

SUMMARY: CHAPTER 15

When the Bulgars attacked the castle, the colonel was left unconscious and appeared dead. He was thrown into a cart full of corpses and taken to a Jesuit chapel for burial. A Jesuit sprinkling holy water on the bodies noticed the colonel's eyes moving, and immediately made arrangements for the colonel's care. After three weeks the colonel recovered completely. Being a "very pretty boy," he earned the "tender friendship" of a highly regarded Jesuit and eventually became a Jesuit himself. He was sent to Paraguay, where he became a colonel as well as a priest.

The colonel hopes to bring Cunégonde to Paraguay. Candide says he wishes to do the same because he plans to marry her. This statement infuriates the colonel, as Candide is not of the nobility.

Candide claims that he agrees with Pangloss's statement that all men are equal, and reminds the colonel how much he has done for Cunégonde and how happily she agreed to marry him. The colonel slaps Candide with his sword, and Candide responds by running the colonel through with his own sword. Candide bursts into tears. Cacambo rushes into the room. He dresses Candide in the colonel's habit, and they flee the pavilion.

SUMMARY: CHAPTER 16

Candide and Cacambo end up in a strange country with no roads. They see two naked women running in a meadow pursued by two monkeys biting at their legs. Candide hopes he can rescue the women and gain their assistance, and so he kills the monkeys. However, instead of being grateful the women fall to the ground and weep over the dead monkeys. Cacambo informs Candide that the monkeys were the women's lovers. Candide and Cacambo hide in a thicket where they fall asleep.

They awaken to find themselves bound and surrounded by a tribe of fierce natives known as Biglugs. The Biglugs rejoice, excited that they are going to get revenge on the Jesuits by eating one. Cacambo tells them in their language that Candide is not a Jesuit. He explains that Candide killed a Jesuit and wore the Jesuit habit to escape. He urges the Biglugs to take the habit to the border and ask the guards to confirm the story. The Biglugs do so and discover that Cacambo is telling the truth. They show Candide and Cacambo the greatest hospitality and accompany them to the edge of their territory. Candide affirms his faith in the perfection of the world.

SUMMARY & ANALYSIS

ANALYSIS: CHAPTERS 14–16

In eighteenth-century Europe, the Americas represented the long-standing promise of a new and brighter future for mankind. The New World attracted clergy in search of converts, merchants in search of riches, and countless adventurers in search of new adventure. In Chapter 10, Candide expresses the hope that the New World is the perfect world Pangloss spoke of, since the Old World clearly is not.

By the eighteenth century, however, the dark side of colonization had already emerged. Educated individuals knew about the horrors of slavery, the oppression of natives, and the diseases spread by inter-cultural contact (of which Pangloss's syphilis is one example).

In these chapters and those that follow, Voltaire portrays the Americas as a region thoroughly corrupted by the vices of the Old World.

The rebellion in Paraguay exposes the hypocrisy and scheming of South American politics. The Jesuit priests lead a revolt of native peoples against the Spanish colonial government, yet the Jesuits are not fighting for the right to self-government for these downtrodden natives. The Biglugs' attitude toward Jesuits makes it clear that the native peoples feel no kinship with the priests who claim to be fighting for them. Instead, the Jesuits merely exploit the rebels in a greedy campaign to grab wealth and power away from the government. The native Paraguayans are the impoverished servants of powerful, wealthy European dissidents, mere pawns in an economic—not ideological—quarrel between Europeans.

In this section, Voltaire seizes another opportunity to mock the hypocrisy of religious leaders and the aristocracy. The colonel tells Candide how a Jesuit priest took him into the order because he found him physically attractive. These leading comments suggest a homosexual relationship between the colonel and his mentor, a situation the Jesuits rigorously and publicly condemned. The colonel's refusal to allow Candide to marry his sister, even after their emigration to America and after hearing all of what Candide has done for Cunégonde, is another example of European aristocratic arrogance.

The description of the Biglugs can be read as a criticism of Jean-Jacques Rousseau's philosophy. Rousseau, another important French Enlightenment thinker, was a bitter rival of Voltaire's. Rousseau viewed man as naturally good and insisted that only the institutions of human civilization, such as property and commerce, corrupt man's innate goodness. He was interested in the figure of the natural man, whom he called the "noble savage." Rousseau held that, in a state of nature without the trappings of civilization, human beings would be ignorant of all vice. Voltaire, conversely, was far more pessimistic about human nature. He describes the Biglugs as men in a state of nature, but they are not noble savages ignorant of vice. Rather, they are filled with the same prejudices and brutality as people from the Old World. Like the Inquisitors in Portugal, they kill people based on their religious affiliation, and like the officers in the city of Azov, they are willing to practice cannibalism.

Cacambo is an interesting exception to Voltaire's bleak view of the New World. Cacambo is of mixed Spanish and Native American ancestry, but he has managed to avoid many of the misfortunes that have befallen both groups in the New World. He deals capably with both the Jesuits and the Biglugs and can speak both native and European languages. He suffers fewer gross misfortunes than any other character, less out of luck than because of his sharp wits, and he proves to be unflaggingly loyal and honest. Though Voltaire does not see hope for a new, better world for the European in the Americas, Cacambo seems to represent a different hope: a new, better man who is neither completely of the Old World nor completely of the New, who bases his personality and ability on his understanding and experience of both worlds.

Though Cacambo inspires optimism in others, he himself is no optimist. His wide experience of the world leads him to the same conclusions as the old woman: he tells the Biglugs that "the law of nature teaches us to kill our neighbor, and that's how men behave the whole world over."

CHAPTERS 17–19

SUMMARY: CHAPTER 17
Cacambo and Candide continue to travel, but their horses die and their food runs out. They find an abandoned canoe and row down a river, hoping to find signs of civilization. After a day, their canoe smashes against some rocks.

Cacambo and Candide make their way to a village, where they find children playing with emeralds, rubies, and diamonds. When the village schoolmaster calls the children, they leave the jewels on the ground. Candide tries to give the jewels to the schoolmaster, but the schoolmaster merely throws them back to the ground.

Cacambo and Candide visit the village inn, which looks like a European palace. The people inside speak Cacambo's native language. Cacambo and Candide eat a grand meal and try to pay for it with two large gold pieces they picked up off the ground. The landlord laughs at them for trying to give him "pebbles." Moreover, the government maintains all inns for free. Candide believes that this is the place in the world where everything is for the best.

SUMMARY: CHAPTER 18
Cacambo and Candide go to see the village sage, a 172-year-old man. The sage explains that his people have vowed never to leave their kingdom, which is called Eldorado. High mountains surround the kingdom, so no outsiders can get in, making Eldorado safe from

European conquests. They also have a God whom they thank every day for giving them what they need. No religious persecution occurs because everyone agrees about everything.

Cacambo and Candide visit the king. They embrace him according to customs explained by one of his servants, and such familiarity and equality of address with a monarch shocks them. Candide asks to see the courts and prisons and learns there are none. Rather, there are schools devoted to the sciences and philosophy.

After a month, Candide decides that he cannot stay in Eldorado as long as Cunégonde is not there. He decides to take as many Eldorado "pebbles" with him as he can. The king considers the plan foolish, but sets his architects to work building a machine to lift Candide, Cacambo, and 102 swift sheep loaded down with jewels out of the deep valley. Candide hopes to pay Don Fernando for Cunégonde and buy a kingdom for himself.

SUMMARY: CHAPTER 19

Cacambo and Candide lose all but two sheep as they travel to Surinam, but the last two sheep still carry a sizable fortune. Cacambo and Candide meet a slave on the road who is missing a leg and a hand. The slave tells them that his own mother sold him to his cruel master, Vanderdendur. He tells them of the misery of slavery, and his words prompt Candide to renounce Pangloss's optimism.

Candide sends Cacambo to retrieve Cunégonde and the old woman. Meanwhile, Candide tries to secure passage to Venice, and Vanderdendur offers his ship. When Candide readily agrees to Vanderdendur's high price, Vanderdendur deduces that Candide's sheep are carrying a fortune. Candide puts his sheep on board in advance, and Vanderdendur sails off without him, taking much of Candide's fortune.

Candide, at great expense, tries but fails to obtain compensation through the legal system. He then books passage on a ship sailing for France and announces that he will pay passage plus a good sum of money to the most unhappy man in the province. Out of the crowd of applicants, Candide chooses a scholar who was robbed by his wife, beaten by his son, and forsaken by his daughter.

———————

ANALYSIS: CHAPTERS 17–19

Eldorado is Voltaire's utopia, featuring no organized religion and no religious persecution. None of the inhabitants attempts to force

SUMMARY & ANALYSIS

beliefs on others, no one is imprisoned, and the king greets visitors as his equals. The kingdom has an advanced educational system and poverty is nonexistent. This world is clearly the best of the worlds represented in *Candide* and seems to be the "best of all possible worlds" in which Pangloss believes.

However, Voltaire's deep pessimism about human nature shines through the glittering portrait of the harmonious, utopian society of Eldorado. The word "utopia," coined by Sir Thomas More in his book of the same name, sounds like the Greek words for both "good place" and "no place." For the suffering inhabitants of the real world, Eldorado might as well not exist. It is almost completely inaccessible from the outside. Riches enough to end world poverty lie untouched on the ground. Its residents refuse to initiate any contact with the outside world because they know that such contact would destroy their perfect country. After some time there, even Candide wants to return immediately to the deeply flawed world outside. The Eldorado "pebbles" will only be of value to him in the outside world. The jewels that make Eldorado beautiful serve to inspire greed and ambition in Candide, whose only previous interests have been survival and his love for Cunégonde.

The fortune that Candide obtains in Eldorado brings him more problems than advantages. He quickly discovers that riches make him into a target for all sorts of swindlers, as Vanderdendur and the Surinamese officers swiftly work to get as much money from Candide as they can. Before he becomes wealthy, Candide still repeatedly finds cause to endorse Pangloss's optimism. After he acquires wealth, however, the fierce blows he suffers shatter his confidence in optimism. Financial injury inspires more pessimism in him than violence ever did. His decision to listen to countless stories of woe and to reward the most miserable man is reminiscent of the old woman's behavior on the trip to America, during which she asked the other passengers to recite their sad tales. This indicates that perhaps Candide identifies more with the old woman's world-weary pessimism now that he has had money. By suggesting that Candide is sorrier to see his money disappear than he was to see his blood shed, Voltaire also comments on the hopeless irrationality of human priorities and on the power of greed.

Candide's attempt to acquire a companion for his voyage reveals the futility of trying to compensate someone for misery and suffering. There are so many miserable people in the world that giving away a little bit of money does virtually nothing to reduce this overall misery. Voltaire implies that the basis for misery is the social structure itself, which needs to be changed before any real compensation can occur.

Candide's new pessimism also owes something to his conversation with the slave whom he encounters on the road to Surinam. Voltaire illustrates social injustice and systematic cruelty many times in the novel. However, many of these situations, such as Candide's conscription into the Bulgar army and the consumption of the old woman's buttock, are exaggerated, absurd, or even comical. The slave's life story, on the other hand, is quite realistic and has no element of humor to it. In dealing with slavery, Voltaire comes up against an evil so powerful that even his considerable satiric wit cannot make light of it.

CHAPTERS 20–23

SUMMARY: CHAPTER 20
Candide still has a little money and a few jewels, and hopes to use what he has to recover Cunégonde. His love and remaining fortune momentarily renew his faith in Pangloss's philosophy. Martin the scholar, on the other hand, maintains that God has abandoned the world because men kill and maim one another everywhere. En route to Bordeaux, Martin and Candide watch a battle between two ships. One ship sinks and its crew perishes. Candide finds his sheep in the water and realizes that the defeated ship belonged to Vanderdendur. Candide claims that there is some good in the world because Vanderdendur has met with just punishment, but Martin asks why Vanderdendur's crew had to die with him.

SUMMARY: CHAPTER 21
When the coast of France is in sight, Candide asks Martin if he has ever been to Paris. Martin says he has, and describes his previous encounters with the French and his disgust at what he calls their lack of manners. Candide asks Martin why the world was made, and Martin replies, "To make us mad." Candide then asks Martin if he believes that men have always done evil things to one another. Martin replies with a question, asking Candide if hawks have always eaten pigeons. When Candide answers yes, Martin counters that if the rest of nature's beasts do not change, then men do not either. Candide disagrees, claiming that men have free will.

SUMMARY: CHAPTER 22

The ship arrives in France, and Candide buys a carriage so that he and Martin can continue to travel together. They decide to visit Paris, but Candide becomes ill upon arriving at their hotel. Candide wears a large diamond on his hand that attracts a great number of new friends, including two physicians, who force their services on him. The physicians only succeed in making Candide sicker. Candide and Martin meet an abbé of Perigord and play cards with him and his friends. The other players cheat, and Candide loses a great deal of money. The abbé takes Candide and Martin to visit the Marquise of Parolignac. While there, Candide argues with a philosopher about whether everything is for the best in this world. The philosopher states that the world is in a state of "unending warfare." The Marquise seduces Candide and steals his jeweled rings.

By manipulating Candide, the abbé learns that Candide has not received a letter from Cunégonde. The next morning, Candide receives a letter signed "Cunégonde" with the news that she is ill in Paris and wishes him to visit her. Candide and Martin are conducted into a dark room. The maidservant explains that Candide may not view Cunégonde because light would be harmful to her. Candide gives diamonds and gold to the woman he believes to be Cunégonde. The abbé arrives with a squad of officers and orders Martin and Candide arrested as "suspicious strangers." Candide bribes an officer with diamonds, and the officer lets them go. The officer's brother, after being given more diamonds, puts Candide and Martin on a ship bound for England.

SUMMARY: CHAPTER 23

When the ship is near shore, Martin and Candide witness the execution of an admiral. They learn that England executes admirals periodically to encourage the rest of the fleet to fight harder, and that this particular admiral was sentenced to death for failing to incite his men to get closer to the enemy during a battle with the French in Canada. Candide refuses to set foot in England and arranges for the captain of the ship to take him to Venice, where he is certain he will be reunited with Cunégonde.

— You see, said Candide to Martin, crime is punished sometimes; this scoundrel of a Dutch merchant has met the fate he deserved. — Yes, said Martin; but did the passengers aboard his ship have to perish too?

(See QUOTATIONS, p. 54)

_____

ANALYSIS: CHAPTERS 20–23

Martin is a foil to Pangloss. He does not believe that everything is for the best in this world, nor does he believe in some natural "good." He acknowledges the evil side of human nature. For Martin, the presence of evil in the world does not inspire convoluted logical justification. Candide tries to counter Martin's arguments by citing the idea of free will. However, free will does not solve the dilemma of the presence of evil in a world created by a perfectly good, omniscient, omnipotent Christian God.

In telling the story of his life, Martin refers to two religious ideologies. He claims that the Surinamese clergy persecuted him because they thought he was a Socinian. The Socinians were a Christian sect formed during the Reformation. They rejected the divinity of Christ, the trinity, and original sin. They greatly influenced Enlightenment thought and aided in the formation of the ideology of the Unitarian Universalist church. The Surinamese clergy were, however, mistaken in their understanding of Martin's "heresy." Martin claims that he is not a Socinian, but a "Manichee." Manichaeism is an ancient religion founded by the sage Mani. The Manichaeans see the universe in terms of the dual forces of good and evil. They believe that these two forces are equally powerful in the world and are continually in conflict. Manichaeans believe that through spiritual knowledge, human beings can conquer the evil side of their natures. Christians, whose doctrines hinge on a belief in a good and all-powerful god who is more powerful than the evil represented by Satan, fiercely reject Manichaeism. The precepts of Manichaeism also directly conflict with Pangloss's optimism, since a world dominated in part by evil cannot be perfect or perfectible.

For the remainder of the novel, Martin's ideas provide an enlightening counterexample to the beliefs espoused by Pangloss and Candide. In general, Martin's arguments seem more reasonable and compelling than Candide's renditions of Pangloss's ideas. But, like Pangloss, Martin believes so firmly in his own view of the world that he occasionally dismisses real evidence that contradicts his philosophy, thereby discrediting it. For example, in Chapter 24, Martin asserts that Cacambo has certainly run off with Candide's money, and according to Martin's cynical opinion of human nature, there is no way Cacambo could do otherwise. In reality, however, Cacambo remains loyal to Candide, even though he does not stand to gain anything. Like Pangloss's optimism, Martin's pessimism is based too heavily on abstract speculation and dogmatic belief, and not enough on empirical evidence. Voltaire personally may have found ideas like Martin's philosophy more credible, but he does not endorse them entirely in his writing. Absolute pessimism, Voltaire seems to say, is as short-sighted and self-defeating as absolute optimism.

In Chapter 22, Voltaire indulges in some relatively good-natured satire of his native country. Voltaire wrote *Candide* after he had been in exile for several years, and his portrait of the Parisian character, while quite condemnatory, has a ring of intimacy to it. He describes the gambling, sexual license, theater, and debauchery of the city in colorful detail. The xenophobia that the abbé exploits to rob Candide and that forces Candide to leave the country is perhaps meant to represent the intellectual intolerance that also forced Voltaire out of his homeland.

Voltaire's portrayal of the English demonstrates the range of his critical eye. He was generally very admiring of English government and culture and considered England the most progressive nation in Europe. However, Voltaire does not attempt to portray England as a perfect, or even a good, place. With his depiction of the admiral's execution, Voltaire acknowledges that even the country he most admires subscribes to the same ridiculous, irrational logic and the same barbaric practices that are found in every other place on earth.

CHAPTERS 24–26

SUMMARY: CHAPTER 24

When Candide fails to find Cunégonde and Cacambo after several months in Venice, he falls into despair. He begins to agree with Martin's claim that the world is misery. Martin scolds Candide for trusting a valet with a fortune of millions, and repeats his argument that there is "little virtue and little happiness on the earth."

On the street, Candide sees a pretty young woman and a young monk walking arm-in-arm with happy expressions on their faces.

When he approaches them, he discovers that the girl is Paquette and the monk is named Brother Giroflée. Paquette, Pangloss's old mistress, confirms Pangloss's story that he caught syphilis from her. A surgeon took pity on Paquette and cured her, and in return she became the surgeon's mistress. The surgeon's jealous wife beat Paquette every day, but the surgeon tired of his wife and poisoned her while treating her for a common cold. His wife's family sued him, so he fled. Paquette was sent to prison but the judge granted her freedom on the condition that she become his mistress. When the judge tired of Paquette he turned her out, and she resorted to prostitution. Brother Giroflée is one of her clients, and Paquette appears happy to please him. Giroflée's parents have forced him into the monastery to increase his older brother's fortune. Giroflée hates the monastery because it is rife with petty intrigue. Candide gives the two money to ease their sorrows.

SUMMARY: CHAPTER 25

Candide visits Count Pococurante in Venice. The wealthy count has a marvelous collection of art and books, but he is unable to enjoy any of it. He finds the paintings of Raphael unpleasant and the works of Homer, Horace, and Milton tiresome. The count once pretended to appreciate these things in front of others, but is now unable to pretend, and scorns those who "admire everything in a well-known author." The count's brashness astonishes Candide, who has never been trained to judge for himself, but Martin finds the count's remarks reasonable. Candide thinks the count must be a genius because nothing pleases him. Martin explains that there is "some pleasure in having no pleasure."

SUMMARY: CHAPTER 26

During Venice's Carnival season, Candide and Martin are dining with six strangers in an inn when they encounter Cacambo, who is now the slave of one of the six strangers. Cacambo explains that Cunégonde is in Constantinople and offers to bring Candide to her. Summoned by his master, he is unable to say any more. Candide and Martin converse with their dinner companions and discover that each is a deposed king from a different corner of Europe. One of them, Theodore of Corsica, is the poorest and least fortunate, and the others each offer him twenty sequins. Candide gives him a diamond worth one hundred times that sum. The kings wonder about his identity and the sources of his generosity.

ANALYSIS: CHAPTERS 24–26

Martin's reaction to Candide's despair at not finding Cunégonde reveals the drawback of his pessimism. Instead of attempting to comfort or even distract his friend and benefactor, Martin gloats over Candide's distress to further confirm his own world-view. Like Pangloss's unqualified optimism, Martin's unqualified pessimism keeps him from taking active steps to improve the world.

Still, that pessimism is further confirmed by the story of Giroflée and Paquette, an apparently blissful young couple whose idyllic appearance masks misfortunes much like those every other character has encountered. Martin warns Candide that throwing money at their problems will not erase them, a warning that bears fruit in the remaining chapters. After all, Candide's wealth has multiplied his problems rather than eliminated them.

The count, who seems to have everything, is still unhappy. He has wealth, education, art, and literature at his command, but none of it truly pleases him. Candide, who had the pleasure of utopia in Eldorado, returned to the imperfect world because he wanted to find Cunégonde and enjoy resources such as those the count has but fails to enjoy. Through the count, who only takes pleasure in constant criticism of everything, Voltaire perhaps means to suggest that human beings are incapable of satisfaction.

In some ways, the count embodies Enlightenment attitudes. The thinkers of that era had access to a greater wealth of art and learning than those of most previous eras of European civilization. The work of the Renaissance artist Raphael and the Greek and Roman authors on the count's bookshelf were important staples of the culture of that period. Yet Enlightenment thinkers were famous for biting criticism. The count voices support for the practice of seeking knowledge and experience before making judgments. He scorns people who judge a writer by his reputation rather than by his work. The emphasis on gaining knowledge through experience is strongly characteristic of Voltaire's own thinking. Thus, it is probable that Voltaire is in some ways sympathetic to the count's critical point of view. The count's discernment certainly seems preferable to Candide's mindless reverence for the authors he has been taught to regard as good. At the same time, the count's character illustrates Voltaire's skepticism at the idea that anything, even great art, can make human beings happy.

The six strangers, who claim to be dethroned kings, serve as an extended mockery of the arrogance of the aristocracy. Although they believe they are naturally endowed with the right to power, they continually lose power through wars and political upheaval. Candide feels sorry for the strangers, but Martin correctly states in Chapter 27 that their sufferings are nothing to shed tears over. The strangers still have valets and slaves at their disposal. One of them even owns Cacambo, Candide's good friend.

The account of the dethroned kings also illustrates the changes that were taking place in Voltaire's society. The growth of capitalism meant that the European nobility was losing influence to commoners who made or acquired wealth of their own accord. The kings wonder at the fact that Candide, a private citizen, has far more money than they do. Voltaire, who was not of noble birth but had a vast fortune, himself lent or gave money to impoverished royals. In this context, the overweening pride of the aristocracy seems not merely unjust but completely unjustified.

CHAPTERS 27–30

SUMMARY: CHAPTER 27

On the way to Constantinople with Cacambo and his master, Candide and Martin learn that Cacambo bought Cunégonde and the old woman from Don Fernando, but that a pirate abducted them and sold them as slaves. Cunégonde has grown horribly ugly, but Candide resolves to love her anyway. Candide purchases Cacambo's freedom. Upon arriving in Turkey, Candide recognizes two galley slaves as the baron and Pangloss. Candide also buys their freedom.

SUMMARY: CHAPTER 28

While the group travels to rescue Cunégonde, the baron and Pangloss tell their stories. The baron bears no ill will toward Candide for stabbing him. After his wound healed, Spanish troops attacked him and sent him to jail in Buenos Aires. The baron eventually returned to Rome to serve his Jesuit order, but was caught bathing naked with a young Turkish man and sent to the galleys.

The executioner who was to hang Pangloss was inexperienced in hangings and made the noose badly, so Pangloss survived. A surgeon bought Pangloss's body for dissection. Pangloss regained consciousness after being cut open, and the startled surgeon sewed him closed again. Pangloss then traveled to Constantinople. He entered

SUMMARY & ANALYSIS

a mosque and saw a pretty young woman drop her nosegay from her bosom. Pangloss picked it up and returned it to her bosom "with the most respectful attentions." Her male companion thought he was taking too long with it, so he had Pangloss arrested. Pangloss was then whipped and sent to the galleys. However, he still believes that pre-established harmony is the "finest notion in the world."

Summary: Chapter 29

Candide purchases the old woman, Cunégonde, and a small farm. Cunégonde reminds Candide of his promise to marry her. Though horrified by her ugliness, Candide does not dare refuse. However, the baron again declares that he will not live to see his sister marry beneath her rank.

Summary: Chapter 30

> I should like to know which is worse, being raped a hundred times by negro pirates ... or ... just sitting here and doing nothing?   (See QUOTATIONS, p. 55)

Pangloss draws up a formal treatise declaring that the baron has no rights over his sister. Martin is in favor of drowning the baron. Cacambo suggests that they return the baron to the galleys without telling Cunégonde, and that is the course they choose.

Cunégonde grows uglier and more disagreeable every day. Cacambo works in the garden of the small farm. He hates the work and curses his fate. Pangloss is unhappy because he has no chance of becoming an important figure in a German university. Martin is patient because he imagines that in any other situation he would be equally unhappy. They all debate philosophy while the misery of the world continues. Pangloss still maintains that everything is for the best but no longer truly believes it. Paquette and Giroflée arrive at the farm, having squandered the money Candide gave them. They are still unhappy, and Paquette is still a prostitute.

The group consults a famous dervish (Muslim holy man) about questions of good and evil. The dervish rebukes them for caring about such questions and shuts the door in their faces. Later, the group stops at a roadside farm. The farmer kindly invites them to a pleasant dinner. He only has a small farm, but he and his family work hard on it and live a tolerable existence.

Candide finds the farmer's life appealing. He, Cunégonde, and his friends decide to follow it, and everyone is satisfied by hard work in the garden. Pangloss suggests to Candide once again that this is the best of possible worlds. Candide responds, "That is very well put . . . but we must cultivate our garden."

ANALYSIS: CHAPTERS 27–30

> —Let's work without speculating, said Martin; it's the only way of rendering life bearable.
>
> (See QUOTATIONS, p. 56)

The far-fetched resurrections of Pangloss and the baron can be read optimistically or pessimistically. On the one hand, two events that gave Candide great grief, the death of his teacher and his own murder of his old friend, have been reversed in an almost miraculous fashion. Candide's most impossible wish has come true. On the other hand, even the fulfillment of that wish brings Candide no real happiness. In fact, the baron actively works to thwart Candide's happiness. Additionally, even near-death experiences and imprisonment have done nothing to alter Pangloss's shallow optimism and the baron's brutish snobbery. Pangloss represents human folly and the baron represents human arrogance, and Voltaire seems to be saying that neither ever really dies.

While Candide's optimism has fluctuated during his travels, Pangloss's has remained static, despite the fact that he has arguably fared far worse than his pupil. Pangloss desires consistency in his thinking, an aspiration that seems rational. However, Pangloss's version of consistency involves an irrational refusal to denounce his excessively optimistic philosophy despite the terrible situations he has encountered. Pangloss no longer even really believes his own words, but he refuses to incorporate his new knowledge into his philosophy. For him, the idea is more important and attractive than reality. The hopeless rigidity of Pangloss's thought is sharply and concisely illustrated by this exchange:

> —Well, my dear Pangloss, Candide said to him, now that you have been hanged, dissected, beaten to a pulp, and sentenced to the galleys, do you still think everything is for the best in this world? —I am still of my first opinion, replied Pangloss; for after all I am a philosopher, and it would not be right for me to recant since

Leibniz could not possibly be wrong, and besides pre-established harmony is the finest notion in the world.

Money, leisure, security, peace, and life with his beloved do not make Candide happy. Martin declares that humans are bound to live "either in convulsions of misery or in the lethargy of boredom." The way out of this dilemma, it seems, lies in the lifestyle of the farmer and in Candide's garden. Candide manages to find a tolerable existence through self-directed improvement and work. Practical action is the only solution Voltaire can find to the problem of human suffering. Each member of the household finds a skill to hone and then uses it to contribute to the support of the household. Without any leisure from their toil in the garden, the characters have no time or energy to trade empty words about good and evil. Candide's new solution seems to alleviate some of their suffering. Pangloss points out that the garden in which everyone finds solace is reminiscent of the biblical Garden of Eden, but there are crucial differences. The characters of *Candide* are ending their adventures in a garden, not beginning them there as Adam and Eve did; and instead of enjoying the free bounty of nature as Adam and Eve did, they must work tirelessly in order to reap any benefits from their garden.

The sincerity of Voltaire's endorsement of this solution is questionable. It seems unlikely that, after having poked malicious fun at countless belief systems, Voltaire should decide to give his readers an unqualified happy ending. The characters finally realize their desires, but misery still reigns in the world outside their garden. Candide and his friends are wealthy and secure—in a perfect position to try to change the world for the better. Yet, rather than engaging the world in an attempt to improve it, they withdraw from it in an attempt to escape their own petty unhappiness. Voltaire, who became very active in political and social causes later in his life, may see withdrawal into a garden as the only wise and viable solution for creatures as weak as human beings. However, it is unlikely that he sees it as the best of all possible solutions.

IMPORTANT QUOTATIONS EXPLAINED

1. Pangloss gave instruction in metaphysico-theologico-cosmolo-nigology. He proved admirably that there cannot possibly be an effect without a cause and that in this best of all possible worlds the baron's castle was the most beautiful of all castles and his wife the best of all possible baronesses. —It is clear, said he, that things cannot be otherwise than they are, for since everything is made to serve an end, everything necessarily serves the best end. Observe: noses were made to support spectacles, hence we have spectacles. Legs, as anyone can plainly see, were made to be breeched, and so we have breeches. . . . Consequently, those who say everything is well are uttering mere stupidities; they should say everything is for the best.

This explanation of Pangloss's optimistic philosophy is quoted from Chapter 1. His philosophy is both the most important point for debate among the novel's characters and one of the main targets of Voltaire's satirical jabs. Pangloss's—and his student Candide's—indomitable belief that human beings live in "the best of all possible worlds" comes under brutal attack by the horrific events that they live through. Their belief broadly resembles the conclusions of a number of the most influential philosophers of Voltaire's time. In particular, the philosopher Leibniz famously maintains that, since the world was created by God, and since the mind of God is the most benevolent and capable mind imaginable, the world must be the best world imaginable. Under such a system, humans perceive evil only because they do not understand the force governing the world and thus do not know that every ill exists only for a greater good. *Candide* is widely thought to be Voltaire's sarcastic retort to Leibniz. In this quotation, Voltaire attacks not only philosophical optimism but also the foibles and errors of Enlightenment philosophy. Enlightenment philosophers such as Leibniz focused a great deal of attention on the interplay of cause and effect. Pangloss's argument about spectacles and breeches demonstrates a ridiculous inability to properly distinguish between cause and effect. Spectacles fit noses not because God created noses to fit spectacles, as Pangloss claims, but the other way around. The obviousness of this point is meant to echo the obviousness of the flaws Voltaire observes in the Enlightenment philosophical process.

2. —A hundred times I wanted to kill myself, but always I loved life more. This ridiculous weakness is perhaps one of our worst instincts; is anything more stupid than choosing to carry a burden that really one wants to cast on the ground? to hold existence in horror, and yet to cling to it? to fondle the serpent which devours us till it has eaten out our heart? —In the countries through which I have been forced to wander, in the taverns where I have had to work, I have seen a vast number of people who hated their existence; but I never saw more than a dozen who deliberately put an end to their own misery.

The old woman, after telling of the rape, slavery, and cannibalism she has experienced, launches into this speculation about suicide in Chapter 12. The question of why more unfortunate people do not kill themselves seems rational in the context of the calamitous, merciless world of the novel. In Voltaire's time, the first and easiest answer should have been that God and Christian doctrine forbid suicide and that those who kill themselves are consigned to spend eternity in hell. However, the old woman's very existence, as an illegitimate child of a Pope, makes a statement against the church, and she does not even consider this approach to the question of suicide. Perhaps the implication is that hell cannot possibly be worse than life, or perhaps the old woman, after her experiences, does not believe in God or an afterlife. The pessimism of this passage is obvious and fairly thorough. The one glimmer of hope that shines through the old woman's words comes from her assertion that people cling to life because they "love" it, not because they are resigned or because they fear eternal punishment. The serpent that is life is not just tolerated but "fondle[d]." Human beings, then, naturally embrace life—a "stupid" move, perhaps, but one that demonstrates passion, strong will, and an almost heroic endurance.

3. The enormous riches which this rascal had stolen were sunk beside him in the sea, and nothing was saved but a single sheep. —You see, said Candide to Martin, crime is punished sometimes; this scoundrel of a Dutch merchant has met the fate he deserved. —Yes, said Martin; but did the passengers aboard his ship have to perish too? God punished the scoundrel, the devil drowned the others.

In Chapter 20, Candide and Martin engage in this debate over the sinking of Vanderdendur's ship. Candide, who tries throughout the novel to find support for Pangloss's optimistic faith in the workings of the world, sees Vanderdendur's fate as a sign that justice is sometimes served by disasters such as shipwrecks, and thus that these disasters serve a higher purpose. Martin, the consummate pessimist, points out quite reasonably that there is no just reason why the other people on Vanderdendur's ship had to die along with him. Martin interprets the event as the product of both God's justice and the devil's cruel mischief. Implied in this statement is the pessimistic idea that the devil's hand is just as evident in the world as God's, and the subversive idea that God and the devil inadvertently cooperate in determining the course of human affairs.

4.   . . . [W]hen they were not arguing, the boredom was
        so fierce that one day the old woman ventured to say:
        —I should like to know which is worse, being raped a
        hundred times by negro pirates, having a buttock cut
        off, running the gauntlet in the Bulgar army, being
        flogged and hanged in an auto-da-fé, being dissected
        and rowing in the galleys—experiencing, in a word,
        all the miseries through which we have passed—or
        else just sitting here and doing nothing? —It's a hard
        question, said Candide. These words gave rise to new
        reflections, and Martin in particular concluded that
        man was bound to live either in convulsions of misery
        or in the lethargy of boredom.

By Chapter 30, Candide and his friends have money, peace, and
security, and Candide has finally married Cunégonde. But, as the old
woman points out, these rare blessings have not brought them happiness. This passage implies that human beings do not suffer only as
a result of political oppression, violent crime, war, or natural disaster. They suffer also from their own intrinsic flaws of chronic bad-
temperedness and restlessness. Up to this point, all of the characters
have been marvelously adept at getting themselves out of difficult or
miserable situations. Faced with boredom in the absence of suffering, however, they cannot seem to find any way out on their own,
and turn to "a very famous dervish" for advice. The one site of
unmixed goodness and joy presented in the novel is the paradise of
Eldorado, which Candide and Cacambo choose to leave. At the
time, their decision to venture back into the world seems unwise. By
this point in the novel, however, the reader wonders in retrospect
whether the plague of boredom would not eventually have afflicted
them in Eldorado as severely as it does in Constantinople. The boredom, as Martin's words emphasize, seems to result not from an
absence of happiness but an absence of suffering.

5.   —You are perfectly right, said Pangloss; for when
      man was put into the garden of Eden, he was put there
      ut operaretur eum, so that he should work it; this
      proves that man was not born to take his ease. —Let's
      work without speculating, said Martin; it's the only
      way of rendering life bearable. The whole little group
      entered into this laudable scheme; each one began to
      exercise his talents. The little plot yielded fine
      crops . . . and Pangloss sometimes used to say to
      Candide: —All events are linked together in the best
      of possible worlds; for, after all, if you had not been
      driven from a fine castle by being kicked in the
      backside for love of Miss Cunégonde, if you hadn't
      been sent before the Inquisition, if you hadn't traveled
      across America on foot, if you hadn't given a good
      sword thrust to the baron, if you hadn't lost all your
      sheep from the good land of Eldorado, you wouldn't
      be sitting here eating candied citron and pistachios.
      —That is very well put, said Candide, but we must go
      and work our garden.

QUOTATIONS

This is the final passage of the novel. The cure for the crushing boredom described in the previous quotation has been found in the hard
work of gardening. As Pangloss points out, this cure recalls the state
of mankind in the garden of Eden, where man was master of all
things. On their small plot of land in Turkey, these characters seem
to have a control over their destinies that they could not achieve in
their lives up until this point. Instead of living at the mercy of cir-
cumstances, they are—literally—reaping what they sow. It is, of
course, surprising that this fictional argument against optimism
should be presented as a happy ending. Given this ending, the reader
might for the first time be inclined to wonder whether Pangloss is
right in claiming to live in "the best of possible worlds." But that
claim and all arguments against it are proscribed by the lifestyle the
characters have discovered. As Candide implies in his final line, gardening leaves no time for philosophical speculation, and everyone is
happier and more productive as a result.

KEY FACTS

FULL TITLE
Candide, or Optimism

AUTHOR
Voltaire (pen name of François-Marie Arouet)

TYPE OF WORK
Novel

GENRE
Satire; adventure novel

LANGUAGE
French

TIME AND PLACE WRITTEN
Schwetzingen, Prussia; and Geneva, Switzerland; 1758–1759

DATE OF FIRST PUBLICATION
January or February, 1759

PUBLISHER
Gabriel Cramer

NARRATOR
Anonymous satirical narrator

POINT OF VIEW
The narrator speaks in the third person, focusing on the perspective and experiences of Candide. Events and characters are described objectively most of the time. Occasionally, they are described as Candide sees them, but this is always done with an ironic tone.

TONE
Ironic; melodramatic

TENSE
Past and present

SETTING (TIME)
1750s

SETTING (PLACE)
Various real and fictional locations in Europe and
South America

PROTAGONIST
Candide

MAJOR CONFLICT
Candide and Pangloss's optimistic world view is challenged
by numerous disasters; Candide's love for Cunégonde is
repeatedly thwarted.

RISING ACTION
Candide is expelled from his home for kissing Cunégonde; he
wanders the world attempting to preserve his life and reunite
with his beloved.

CLIMAX
Candide finds Cunégonde enslaved in Turkey; the two
are married.

FALLING ACTION
Candide, Cunégonde, Pangloss, and their friends struggle with
boredom; they find solace in gardening.

THEMES
The folly of optimism; the uselessness of philosophical
speculation; the hypocrisy of religion; the corrupting power
of money

MOTIFS
Resurrection; rape; political oppression

SYMBOLS
Pangloss; the garden; the Lisbon earthquake

FORESHADOWING
There is virtually no foreshadowing in this wildly chaotic
narrative. Candide's repeated musings about what Pangloss
would think of events foreshadows Pangloss's "resurrection."

STUDY QUESTIONS & ESSAY TOPICS

STUDY QUESTIONS

1. *What is the relationship between Candide's adventures and Pangloss's teachings?*

Candide represents an extended criticism of the ideas of the seventeenth-century philosopher Leibniz. Voltaire casts Pangloss as a satirical representation of Leibniz. Leibniz conceptualized the world in terms of a pre-determined harmony, claiming that evil exists only to highlight good and that this world is the best possible world because God created it. Leibniz's concept of the world is part of a larger school of thought called theodicy, which attempts to explain the existence of evil in a world created by an omniscient, omnipotent, perfectly good God. Voltaire criticizes this school for its undiluted optimism. If this is the best possible world, his story suggests, then why should anyone try to alleviate suffering? Pangloss is also a parody of an excessively abstract philosopher. Voltaire scorned philosophers who did not base their arguments on knowledge gathered from a study of the world. Pangloss talks about the structure of the world, but knows little about it since he has lived an idle life inside a castle. Candide believes Pangloss's philosophy without question because he has never had any direct experiences with the outside world.

Candide's adventures begin with his expulsion from the castle. The series of misfortunes that befall him serve as a re-education via direct experience with the world. His experiences in the real world directly contradict Pangloss's optimism. In reality, the world is a terrible place full of evil, cruelty and suffering. Thus, Candide and the reader are forced to reject optimism. Still, the novel does not conclude in favor of absolute pessimism either. Candide eventually finds happiness in hard work and rejects all questions of good and evil or optimism and pessimism. It is only when Candide gives up adventures in travel, love, and philosophy that he discovers happiness in tending his garden.

2. *Is Voltaire's portrait of Eldorado optimistic or*
pessimistic? Why?

Eldorado is a utopia—an imaginary perfect world. Candide decides
that it is the "best of all possible worlds" that Pangloss has taught
him to believe in. Eldorado does not suffer from religious persecution, petty squabbles, or social inequality. Thus, Voltaire is optimistically proposing that human beings are capable of creating a just,
peaceful society. At the same time, the kingdom is almost inaccessible to outsiders, and its king explains that that is the only way it can
remain perfect. Thus, a good society is attainable only if it excludes
the vast majority of humanity. In addition, the jewels and gold that
litter the streets of Eldorado activate common greed in Candide,
who has displayed little lust for money prior to entering the kingdom. Rather than remain in Eldorado, where the jewels are of no
value, Candide elects to return to the flawed outside world where
they will make him rich. For him, the prospect of being wealthy in
an imperfect society is preferable to the prospect of being an average
man in a perfect society. Voltaire's portrait of Eldorado is not pessimistic; rather, he uses Eldorado to convey a pessimistic portrait of
human nature.

3. *What is the significance of Candide's retreat to his garden at the end of the novel? Does he find a credible solution to the problems and evils he has experienced?*

In his garden, Candide manages to find a tolerable existence through self-directed improvement and work. Practical action seems to be the only way to eliminate human suffering. Each member of Candide's household finds a skill to hone and then uses it to contribute to the support of the household. Without any leisure from their toil in the garden, the characters have no time or energy to trade empty words about good and evil.

Candide's garden does seem to alleviate his and his friends' suffering, but the sincerity of Voltaire's endorsement of this solution is questionable. The characters have finally attained happiness, but their previous experiences remind the reader that misery still reigns in the world outside their garden. Candide and his friends are wealthy and secure—in a perfect position to try to change the world for the better. Yet, rather than engaging the world in an attempt to improve it, they withdraw from it in an attempt to escape their own petty unhappiness. Voltaire, who was himself quite active in political and social causes, might view withdrawal into a garden as a wise and viable solution for the problems arising from human weakness, but it is unlikely that he saw it as the best of all possible solutions to the misery in the world.

SUGGESTED ESSAY TOPICS

1. Discuss the significance of Jacques' character. How does he fit in with Voltaire's general view of human nature? What is the significance of his death?

2. The old woman has thought about suicide "a hundred times" but has refused to end her life. Why might that be?

3. Martin claims that people "live either in convulsions of misery or in the lethargy of boredom." Do the events of the novel support that statement? Is one of the two options worse than the other? If what Martin says is true, what does it imply about the value of social change and political activism?

4. How do the experiences of the women in *Candide* differ from those of the men? How do their reactions to those experiences differ from those of the men?

5. What does Voltaire think about European colonization of the Americas? Discuss the significance of the character of Cacambo and of Candide's encounter with the slave.

6. Does Voltaire agree with Martin's outlook on the world? Why or why not?

REVIEW & RESOURCES

QUIZ

1. Why is Candide expelled from the baron's castle?

   A. For arguing with Pangloss
   B. For kissing Cunégonde
   C. For catching syphilis from Paquette
   D. For poaching on the baron's lands

2. What is Jacques' religious affiliation?

   A. Anabaptist
   B. Catholic
   C. Atheist
   D. Jewish

3. Which of the old woman's body parts was eaten by soldiers in a besieged fort?

   A. Her arm
   B. Her breast
   C. Her cheek
   D. Her buttock

4. Whom does the Jesuit commander turn out to be?

   A. Pangloss
   B. Cunégonde's brother, the baron
   C. Cunégonde's father
   D. Cunégonde's ex-lover

5. What is the name of the hidden country into which Candide and Cacambo stumble?

   A. Eldorado
   B. Shangri-la
   C. Utopia
   D. Panglea

6. Which of the following institutions *does* the abovementioned country have?

   A. Prisons
   B. Schools
   C. Churches
   D. Bawdy houses

7. Which Enlightenment thinker is Pangloss's character meant to satirize?

   A. Jean-Jacques Rousseau
   B. Blaise Pascal
   C. Alexander Pope
   D. Gottfried Wilhelm von Leibniz

8. How do Candide and Cacambo escape from the Biglugs?

   A. Candide offers them money
   B. Cacambo reasons with them in their own language
   C. Candide introduces them to Pangloss's optimism
   D. Candide and Cacambo claim to have syphilis

9. What precious animal does Vanderdendur steal from Candide?

   A. A prize-winning racehorse
   B. A sheep laden with jewels
   C. A talking cow
   D. A goose that lays golden eggs

10. Of what religious affiliation is Martin?

    A. Atheist
    B. Buddhist
    C. Manichean
    D. Zoroastrian

11. Why is the English admiral executed?

    A. For fighting too prudently
    B. For betraying state secrets
    C. For sexually harassing his superior's wife
    D. For being a homosexual

12. With whom did Voltaire eventually share a tomb?

   A. Gottfried Wilhelm von Leibniz
   B. Rene Descartes
   C. King Frederick of Prussia
   D. Jean-Jacques Rousseau

13. Which of the following authors does Count Pococurante *not* disparage?

   A. Homer
   B. Milton
   C. Horace
   D. Shakespeare

14. Where does Candide find Pangloss and the baron?

   A. In a Turkish brothel
   B. At a Christian mission in Turkey
   C. At a German university
   D. In a Turkish chain gang

15. What activity brings Candide pleasure at the end of the novel?

   A. Carpentry
   B. Gardening
   C. Sailing
   D. Fencing

16. About what event did Voltaire write a long poem?

   A. The Lisbon earthquake of 1755
   B. The execution of John Byng
   C. The death of Louis XIV
   D. The Seven Years' War

17. The Enlightenment is also known as what?

   A. The Age of Incredulity
   B. The Technology Age
   C. The Age of Reason
   D. The Renaissance

REVIEW & RESOURCES

18. Why will the baron not allow Candide to marry Cunégonde?

    A. Because Candide is a commoner
    B. Because Candide ran the baron through with his sword
    C. Because the baron secretly lusts after Cunégonde
    D. Because the baron suspects that Candide is Jewish

19. Who owns the unfortunate slave whom Candide encounters in Surinam?

    A. Don Fernando
    B. The Pope
    C. Jacques
    D. Vanderdendur

20. Cunégonde has been the mistress of all of the following characters except one. Which one?

    A. Don Isaachar
    B. Cacambo
    C. The Grand Inquisitor
    D. The Bulgar officer

21. In which city are Martin and Candide arrested for being "suspicious strangers"?

    A. Venice
    B. Lisbon
    C. Amsterdam
    D. Paris

22. Which character maintains that this is "the best of all possible worlds"?

    A. Martin
    B. Pangloss
    C. Cunégonde
    D. Jacques

23. To which of the following is Pangloss not subjected?

    A.   Cannibalism
    B.   Syphilis
    C.   Hanging
    D.   Dissection

24. Which character is dead at the end of the novel?

    A.   Cunégonde
    B.   Jacques
    C.   The baron
    D.   Pangloss

25. What does Candide do to the deposed king Theodore of Corsica?

    A.   Makes him his slave
    B.   Gives him a diamond
    C.   Preaches to him about the equality of mankind
    D.   Uses him as a social crutch

REVIEW & RESOURCES

Answer Key:
1: B; 2. A; 3: D; 4: B; 5: A; 6: B; 7: D; 8: B; 9: B; 10: C;
11. A; 12: D; 13: D; 14: D; 15: B; 16: A; 17: C; 18: A; 19: D;
20: B; 21: D; 22: B; 23: A; 24: B; 25: B

SUGGESTIONS FOR FURTHER READING

BOTTIGLIA, WILLIAM F., ed. *Voltaire: A Collection of Critical Essays.* Englewood Cliffs, New Jersey: Prentice, 1968.

CROCKER, LESTER G. *An Age of Crisis: Man and World in Eighteenth Century French Thought.* Baltimore: Johns Hopkins University Press, 1959.

KEENER, FREDERICK. *The Chain of Becoming: The Philosophical Tale, the Novel, and a Neglected Realism of the Enlightenment.* New York: Columbia University Press, 1983.

LEIBNIZ, GOTTFRIED WILHELM VON. *Essays of Theodicy on the Goodness of God, the Freedom of Man and the Origin of Evil.* Trans. F.M. Huggard. Ed. Austin Farrer. London: Routledge, 1952.

MASON, HAYDN. CANDIDE: *Optimism Demolished.* New York: Twayne Publishers, 1992.

RIDGEWAY, RONALD S. *Voltaire and Sensibility.* Montreal: McGill-Queens University Press, 1973.

WADE, IRA. *Voltaire and* CANDIDE: *A Study in the Fusion of History, Art, and Philosophy.* Princeton: Princeton University Press, 1959.

WORCESTER, DAVID. *The Art of Satire.* Cambridge: Harvard University Press, 1940.

A NOTE ON THE TYPE

The typeface used in SparkNotes study guides is Sabon, created by master typographer Jan Tschichold in 1964. Tschichold revolutionized the field of graphic design twice: first with his use of asymmetrical layouts and sanserif type in the 1930s when he was affiliated with the Bauhaus, then by abandoning assymetry and calling for a return to the classic ideals of design. Sabon, his only extant typeface, is emblematic of his latter program: Tschichold's design is a recreation of the types made by Claude Garamond, the great French typographer of the Renaissance, and his contemporary Robert Granjon. Fittingly, it is named for Garamond's apprentice, Jacques Sabon.

.

SparkNotes Study Guides:

SPARKNOTES
TEST PREPARATION
GUIDES

The SparkNotes team figured it was time to cut standardized tests down to size. We've studied the tests for you, so that SparkNotes test prep guides are:

Smarter:
Packed with critical-thinking skills and test-
taking strategies that will improve your score.

Better:
Fully up to date, covering all new features of the tests,
with study tips on every type of question.

Faster:
Our books cover exactly what you need to
know for the test. No more, no less.

SparkNotes Guide to the SAT & PSAT
SparkNotes Guide to the SAT & PSAT — Deluxe Internet Edition
SparkNotes Guide to the ACT
SparkNotes Guide to the ACT — Deluxe Internet Edition
SparkNotes Guide to the SAT II Writing
SparkNotes Guide to the SAT II U.S. History
SparkNotes Guide to the SAT II Math Ic
SparkNotes Guide to the SAT II Math IIc
SparkNotes Guide to the SAT II Biology
SparkNotes Guide to the SAT II Physics

SAT and PSAT are registered trademarks of the College Entrance Examination Board, which does not endorse these books.
ACT is a registered trademark of ACT, Inc. which neither sponsors nor endorses these books.